The Vision
Of Peace

To Dale,
Lovely to meet
you.

Síocháin,

Peace,

Mairead Maguire
2· 11· 2001.

The Vision Of Peace

Faith and Hope in Northern Ireland

Mairead Corrigan Maguire

Edited by John Dear

ORBIS BOOKS

Maryknoll, New York 10545

The Catholic Foreign Mission Society of America (Maryknoll) recruits and trains people for overseas missionary service. Through Orbis Books, Maryknoll aims to foster the international dialogue that is essential to mission. The books published, however, reflect the opinions of their authors and are not meant to represent the official position of the society.

Copyright © 1999 by Mairead Corrigan Maguire

Published by Orbis Books, Maryknoll, NY 10545-0308, USA

Grateful acknowledgment is made to *Parade* magazine for permission to reprint "A Mother Pleads for Peace" © 1985.

Queries regarding rights and permissions should be addressed to: Orbis Books, P.O. Box 308, Maryknoll, NY 10545-0308.

Manufactured in the United States of America

Library of Congress Cataloging-in-Publication Data
Maguire, Mairead Corrigan.
    The vision of peace : faith and hope in Northern Ireland / Mairead
Corrigan Maguire ; edited by John Dear.
        p.   cm.
    ISBN 1-57075-251-6
    1. Northern Ireland – Politics and government – 1994-
2. Nonviolence – Religious aspects – Christianity. 3. Peace
movements – Northern Ireland. 4. Peace movements. I. Dear, John,
1959-   . II. Title.
DA990.U46M364   1999
320.9416–dc21   98-32005

For my husband, Jackie,
my beloved sister Anne,
our children, Mark, Joanne,
Marie-Louise, John, and Luke,
and my mother, Margaret.
With all my love.
Deo Gratias.

LISTEN

Take time to listen to the birds,
the waves,
the wind.

Take time to breathe in the air,
the earth,
the ocean.

Take time to be still,
to be silent,
to allow God to fill you up
with deep peace and love.

— MAIREAD CORRIGAN MAGUIRE

Contents

Part III
PEACE FOR ALL HUMANITY

Preface

The Dalai Lama

In our increasingly small and interdependent world there is an ever more urgent need to bring about genuine world peace. Everyone wishes to live in peace, but it is not achieved by merely talking or thinking about it, nor by waiting for someone else to do something about it. We each have to take responsibility as best as we can within our own sphere of activity.

I, therefore, greatly admire the efforts being made by my friend Mairead Corrigan Maguire towards spreading the message of peace.

Concerned groups and individuals everywhere have a responsibility to work for peace. We have an obligation to promote a new vision of society. One in which war has no place in resolving disputes among states, communities, or individuals, but in which nonviolence is the preeminent value in all human relations.

The key to genuine world peace, however, is inner peace, and the foundation of that is a sense of understanding and respect for each other as human beings, based on compassion and love. Some may dismiss love and compassion as impractical and unrealistic, but I believe their practice is the true source of success.

Compassion is, by nature, peaceful and gentle, but it is also very powerful. It is a sign of true inner strength. To achieve it we do not need to become religious, nor do we need any ideology. All that is necessary is for us to develop our fundamental human qualities such as caring for others, respecting them, and being just and honest.

Foreword

Archbishop Desmond Tutu

I can almost hear myself intoning from the pulpit, "We can each make a difference." I am sure most of us have heard this exhortation ad nauseam and wondered who could deliver us from bondage to this apparent cliché.

But cliché or not, it does in fact happen to be true, and we have in Mairead Corrigan Maguire an outstanding, indeed almost spectacular, example of one individual who has indeed made a difference.

We often hear people say, "Oh, I'm just an ordinary this or that...." I have frequently had to say there is in our theology no such thing as an "ordinary this or that." We are all quite special since we are each that marvelous creation, a person created in the image of God. For that reason, we are each a God-carrier, God's viceroy, God's representative. That makes each one of us truly special.

Let us speak conventionally and say in Mairead we have what would in everyday parlance be described as an "ordinary housewife." Wow, what an "ordinary housewife" she has turned out to be!

Outraged as others were by the mindless carnage in her beloved Northern Ireland since the Troubles began in 1969, but particularly appalled at the needless deaths of her two nephews and one niece — three little children — and the injuring of their mother, her sister Anne, in August 1976, she galvanized thousands of people to take part in weekly peace marches and demonstrations to say, "Enough is enough!" to the violence that has wracked her native land. Together with Betty Williams, Ciaran McKeown, and others, she spearheaded demonstrations that saw half a million people take to the streets in Northern Ireland, England, and Eire. Together, they founded the Community of the Peace People.

This was a tremendous job in a country torn apart by sectarian strife and animosity, where processions could set off further violence and killings. It called forth considerable courage to work for peace when so many seemed to delight in baying for blood and spewing forth hate and intolerance.

It was fitting that Betty Williams and Mairead Corrigan Maguire should have been jointly awarded the Nobel Peace Prize for 1976, and they have not allowed the grass to grow under their feet. They have often, together with other Nobel laureates, shown that the world is their parish as they have been involved in global issues of peace, justice, disarmament, the empowerment of women, and the protection of children.

Mairead Corrigan Maguire has amazed me as I have watched her with growing admiration. She belongs to the world as she has become more and more consistently an advocate for world peace and disarmament, because more and more she has understood the gospel of Jesus to demand that his followers should be nonviolent, pacifists, that they should refuse to use violence to advance their cause. She has demonstrated cogently that it is an obscenity to spend such staggering amounts on budgets for death and destruction when a minute fraction of these budgets would ensure that God's children everywhere would have enough to eat, adequate housing, affordable and accessible health care, and a safe and secure environment, and that they would be able to enjoy childhood. It is unacceptable that so many children and adults go to bed hungry every night and many thousands die from preventable deficiency diseases when their impoverished nations squander scarce resources on procuring arms which are as often as not used not to defend them but to harass and oppress and intimidate them.

Mairead finds it quite intolerable that the affluent West can happily see much of the aid it gives to the developing world return in the form of payment for unnecessary arms. She is equally passionate about the immorality of the international debt burden and would wish to see the biblical principles of the Jubilee Year applied to this situation, so that debts are forgiven and indebted people are given the opportunity to make a new beginning without the debilitating encumbrance of the debt.

She has herself been inspired by some wonderful people and she joins that select band who are a source of inspiration to others who declare that there is indeed a light at the end of the tunnel.

It is because she has tried to make a difference that the world can give thanks today that there has been a Good Friday Agreement, that there have been a successful referendum and elections, and that peace is being given a real chance in Northern Ireland.

Thanks be to God for God's servant Mairead, the "ordinary housewife" who turned out to be anything but ordinary.

1976 peace rally on Shankill Road, Belfast.

Introduction

John Dear, S.J.

Along the busy Lisburn Road in war-ravaged Belfast, Northern Ireland, stands a wee house dedicated to peace. A bright yellow banner hangs outside the second-floor window: "Campaign for a Gun-Free Northern Ireland." Inside, ordinary women and men, young and old, believers from all faiths and non-believers, carry on a steady, persistent witness for peace and justice. Pictures of peacemakers and heroes, such as Martin Luther King, Jr., Gandhi, and Aung San Suu Kyi (the Nobel Peace Prize winner from Burma), line the house walls, an ever-present "cloud of witnesses" watching over their shoulders.

One picture in particular catches my attention. Above the mantelpiece in the spacious front room hangs a large picture from a 1976 Belfast demonstration featuring thousands of women with banners calling for an end to violence and a new day of peace for Northern Ireland. While living and working in Northern Ireland in 1997–98, I used to visit Peace House and look in amazement at that picture.

Belfast, 1976! The height of "the Troubles." From 1969 to 1998, over thirty-four hundred people were killed in a brutal war stemming from British colonial interests, revolutionary republicanism, and age-old, oppressive religious bigotry and fanaticism. But after a year of tumultuous political negotiations, a breakthrough settlement was reached on Good Friday 1998, bringing Northern Ireland to the Easter dawn of peace. Suddenly, what was once deemed unimaginable, unthinkable, indeed impossible, is now indeed possible and probable. A new future stands on the horizon of Ireland — a vision of peace.

As that 1976 photograph testifies, thousands of ordinary people throughout Northern Ireland, mainly women, have been calling for an end to the killings and a future of peace since the Troubles began. The 1976 "Peace People" movement organized the largest nonviolent demonstrations in the history of Northern Ireland — at the time of the greatest number of killings. At the heart of this courageous peace movement stood a young woman named Mairead Corrigan Maguire.

Mairead was thrust into a leadership position in the wake of tragedy. On August 10, 1976, two of her nephews and one of her nieces, all little children, were killed on a Belfast street corner. A British army patrol shot and killed an IRA gunman, Danny Lennon, whose car then plowed into the sidewalk, killing the children, and severely injuring Mairead's sister Anne, who died several years later. In a land soaked with blood, their deaths came as a severe shock. Suddenly, thousands of people began to say, "Enough is enough. The killing and violence have to stop." With Betty Williams and Ciaran McKeown, Mairead organized weekly peace marches and demonstrations that instantly brought out over half a million people throughout Northern Ireland, as well as in England and Ireland. They also co-founded the Community of the Peace People to continue their peacemaking initiatives. The following year Betty and Mairead were awarded the 1976 Nobel Peace Prize. (In 1976 the prize was not awarded. In October 1977 Betty and Mairead were told they had received the 1976 prize, while Amnesty International received the 1977 prize. Both prizes were awarded at the same ceremony in Oslo, Norway, in December 1977.)

But just as quickly the media interest evaporated, the peace demonstrators went back home — and the war raged on. With quiet determination, Mairead continued her work for peace. While all about seemed possessed with violence, she spoke the unpopular word — *nonviolence*. Since 1976, Mairead has insisted "that a peaceful and just society can be achieved only through nonviolent means and that the path to peace lies in each of our hearts." That means no more violence, no more killings, no more injustice, no more death. With prayerful conviction, she stood on the streets of Belfast and said No — No to the IRA, No to the UDA and LVF (the Ulster Defence Association and the Loyalist Volunteer Force, unionist/loyalist paramilitaries), No to the British government's emergency laws and interrogation centers and human rights abuses, No to injustice, bigotry, discrimination, No to any desecration of human life and dignity.

With her friends, Mairead organized nonviolent actions, spoke out against war, reconciled peoples on both sides of the dividing wall, and said Yes to a vision of peace for Northern Ireland and the whole world. Everywhere she went, she spread her gentle, life-giving, disarming spirit.

In Belfast, where Catholics and Protestants still walk on opposite sides of the streets, where the long memory of past bloodshed keeps the demonic spirit of vengeance alive, where retaliation is too often the principal topic of conversation over a pint of Guinness at the corner pub, Mairead's vision of nonviolence was not well received, particularly in the 1980s and early 1990s. She was dismissed, ridiculed, and ignored, while those who called for vengeance and violence found an audience.

But Mairead has remained faithful. She continues in her quiet, gentle way to announce a vision of peace, even in the face of violence, resentment, and rage. Right from the beginning, long before the Good Friday 1998 peace agreement, she understood that such a vision had to stretch beyond the narrow boundaries of the six counties of the North and embrace a nonviolent future for all humanity.

"I believe that hope for the future depends on each of us taking nonviolence into our hearts and minds and developing new and imaginative structures which are nonviolent and life-giving for all," Mairead writes. "Some people will argue that this is too idealistic. I believe it is very realistic. I am convinced that humanity is fast evolving to this higher consciousness. For those who say it cannot be done, let us remember that humanity learned to abolish slavery. Our task now is no less than the abolition of violence and war.... We can rejoice and celebrate today because we are living in a miraculous time. Everything is changing and everything is possible."

"If we want to reap the harvest of peace and justice in the future," Mairead says, "we will have to sow seeds of nonviolence, here and now, in the present."

Since 1976, Mairead has been sowing seeds of nonviolence throughout Northern Ireland and the world. This book gathers together for the first time her story and her message of nonviolence for Northern Ireland and the world.

Part I, "Peace in Northern Ireland," includes reflections on the history of the Peace People movement and the death of her family members; her open letters to the IRA and Gerry Adams; her call for "a politics of mercy and forgiveness"; her thoughts on the role of Irish women in the struggle for peace; and her well-publicized letter to her son Luke (first published in *Parade* magazine in 1985, to widespread acclaim).

Part II, "Peace in the World," includes her reflections on Gandhi and nonviolence; her pilgrimages to Auschwitz, the former Yugoslavia, and Hiroshima; the need for peace and justice in East Timor and Nigeria; the imperative of nuclear disarmament; and her nomination of antiwar activists Daniel and Philip Berrigan for the Nobel Peace Prize.

The last section, Part III, "Peace for All Humanity," includes broader reflections on the future of the planet; the church's vocation to make peace; and her campaign with twenty other Nobel Peace Prize winners to call for a new millennium dedicated to teaching nonviolence.

As Northern Ireland emerges from its bloodbath and commits itself to a future of peace, the rest of us do well to ponder the wisdom of this persistent, gentle visionary, a wisdom born out of pain and bloodshed, in the hope that we too might learn to see the way to peace.

In a time of widespread blindness, when people cannot see clearly because of the wounds of violence and division, Mairead offers a new vision, the possibility of nonviolence.

In this book, Mairead offers the lens of nonviolence as the key to envisioning a new millennium of peace and justice. Through these peace spectacles, we see ourselves as we are, already reconciled, all of us equal sisters and brothers of one another, children of the God of peace.

For Mairead's faithful nonviolence, we can only offer our gratitude — and our pledge to pursue this vision into the future.

I

Peace in Northern Ireland

*Betty Williams and Mairead Corrigan Maguire reading the Peace
Declaration at the Shankill Road rally in 1976.*

1

The Story of Peace People

The Peace People movement was born out of the tragic deaths of sixteen hundred people during the first seven years of "the Troubles" in Northern Ireland. The particular tragedy that brought people finally, in desperation, onto the streets in Northern Ireland was the death of three children on August 10, 1976. They were my sister Anne's children, Joanne (eight and a half years old), John (two and a half years old), and Andrew (six weeks old). They died when a British army patrol shot and killed a nineteen-year-old IRA volunteer, Danny Lennon, whose car then crashed onto the sidewalk along Finaghy Road North in Belfast, killing my sister's children and seriously injuring her.

The people of Northern Ireland, already grieved at the death of so many people, were deeply moved by these further deaths. Within weeks, tens of thousands of people took part in demonstrations throughout Northern Ireland demanding an end to the violence.

The children were buried on Friday, August 13, at Milltown Cemetery in Belfast, and on that day I met for the first time my friends Ciaran McKeown and Betty Williams. Ciaran was a well-known journalist and a dedicated pacifist. Betty, a mother from Belfast, had responded to these deaths by immediately organizing a petition against the senseless violence.

On Saturday, August 14, ten thousand people gathered on Finaghy Road North, Belfast, to express their longing for peace. A few days later, Betty, Ciaran, and I met again and decided to join together to work for peace. Even though the three of us were so different, we felt an immediate bond between us, and at the heart of that bond was trust. Later that day, we agreed to call our movement the Peace People. Ciaran borrowed the blue exercise book I had been using to jot down names and numbers and wrote out "The Declaration of the

---

An address to the Peace People Assembly, October 18, 1986, at Benburb, Northern Ireland.

Peace People," which we read at every rally and gathering from then on:

> We have a simple message for the world from this movement for peace.

> We want to live and love and build a just and peaceful society.

> We want for our children, as we want for ourselves, our lives at home, at work, and at play, to be lives of joy and peace.

> We recognize that there are many problems in society which are a source of conflict and violence. We recognize that every bullet fired and every exploding bomb makes that work more difficult.

> We reject the use of the bomb and the bullet and all the techniques of violence.

> We dedicate ourselves to working with our neighbors, near and far, day in and day out, to building that peaceful society in which the tragedies we have known are a bad memory and a continuing warning.

The next day we announced the Ormeau Park rally for Saturday, August 21. Over fifty thousand people from all over Northern Ireland marched in the largest peace demonstration ever.

Each Saturday for the next four months we organized rallies throughout Northern Ireland. Thousands of people, particularly women, traveled from all over to attend these rallies calling for an end to the violence. It has been calculated, even allowing for those who might have attended several or all of the demonstrations, North and South, that one in ten of Ireland's entire population marched for peace in the autumn of 1976. That is the most conservative estimate: the figure has been put as high as 750,000, almost twice as many. Some people would organize their own buses. I well remember hopping from bus to bus, and even when I was physically tired, the singing and laughter on the buses never failed to lift my spirit.

I remember the sunny day, August 28, when over twenty-five thousand of us walked along the Shankill Road, the loyalist/Protestant neighborhood. Before this march, I received a telephone call from a nun asking me if she and some of the other nuns should come to the march wearing their religious habits or in ordinary clothes. They came in their habits, and we will never forget those nuns being hugged and welcomed by the people of the Shankill. Their welcome was indeed warmer than the sun.

That same day, over fifty thousand people marched in solidarity with us in Dublin.

The Falls Road rally is another important memory for me. Thousands marched along the Falls, and at one point some people threw stones at us and attacked us. My sister Anne had recovered slightly from her injuries and had only recently learned to walk again. She insisted on coming to the rally to read the Declaration of the Peace People. I will never forget her enormous courage as she stood in pain and in the cold rain to read the declaration.

There were many rallies in the South of Ireland, and these ended at the River Boyne. At the first of these, as we came onto the bridge, the mist which had been covering it rose into the air, and we faced each other for the first time. There was a great rush forward and people from the North and the South began laughing and hugging each other.

There were also rallies held throughout Britain, and these ended with the final rally in London. Joan Baez called and asked to join us. I remember her clear, beautiful voice rising out over the crowd in Trafalgar Square as she sang "We Shall Overcome."

For the first three weeks of the Peace People, we operated from Betty's home. The telephone never stopped ringing, and we were helped by a number of early volunteers to answer the phone from the beginning of the day to the end. We told those calling where and when the next rally would be, and we asked them, if they could, to start a peace group in their own area. On an old gray folder I wrote, "September 16, 1976 — 66 peace groups." Right from the start, people knew that the rallies would end in December and that the work would continue through the efforts of community groups after that.

We asked these newly formed groups to do whatever they felt was needed for peace in their own local community and then to travel out to meet and make new friends in other communities. They were also asked to break down the barriers of fear by going where people were usually afraid to go. They did this regularly and with great courage.

It was a time of heroic effort and fast learning for many people in over a hundred groups. And yet, for whatever reasons, over time, most of those groups folded up. I certainly know why the Falls Road group, which I belonged to, ended. We were eventually refused the use of the premises where we met because we were "too political."

The very word "political" caused conflict within the Peace People movement. Some felt that integrated projects (bringing together Catholics and Protestants, nationalists and unionists) should be our priority and that if we involved ourselves in anything controversial, we would find it difficult to raise money, as well as to develop our reconciliation work. Others argued that without justice there can be no real peace, and so for years some people spoke out against interrogation methods and other injustices under the Emergency Provisions Act. For instance, people were being convicted and sentenced to life in prison solely on the basis of confessions signed while they were in custody and being interrogated under the Emergency Provisions Act.

There was, and perhaps always will be, tension between these aspects of peacemaking — the need for justice and the need for reconciliation. It is to the great credit of the grassroots members of Peace People that our annual assemblies always voted to serve both needs. Peace People worked to create opportunities for meeting, dialogue, and reconciliation and, at the same time, worked for a just judicial process and just structures. The Peace People believe that working nonviolently for reconciliation and justice is the way forward to peace in Northern Ireland and in the world.

This way forward connects us with people working nonviolently for change in other parts of the world. It became natural for us to travel and give support and encouragement to others. One of my outstanding memories is of my trip to Argentina to support the nonviolent human rights activist Adolfo Pérez Esquivel. He was under house arrest at the time but courageously insisted on accompanying me, and as we traveled around I was conscious of how difficult it is to work for peace in many other countries. Anything we can do to support the fragile network of friends and communities around the world working for a nonviolent human family we must do.

⚭

Dealing with local and international media, visiting schools and groups, traveling here and there, attending committee meetings, board meetings, and assemblies, and answering correspondence from around the world all added up to incredible pressures. Though we were sometimes inefficient, we managed for the most part to cope well under the circumstances.

It is all the more amazing when you think that most of our members were ordinary women who had little or no experience with philosophical ideas or political organizing. I remember speaking at a Peace People assembly in the splendid surroundings of the Europa Hotel in Belfast and my legs going to jelly as I watched the colored lights going on and off in front of me. I was so frightened by it all that I asked Ciaran to give the talk instead, but he promptly told me that I must get up and speak. Hard as those days were for all of us, I believe it was a time of growth for us all.

In the first two months, Ciaran McKeown founded our newspaper, *Peace by Peace,* and by the spring of 1977 we had a twelve-page fortnightly which offered an opening onto the doorsteps of homes in the towns and villages throughout Northern Ireland and the world. Funds from the Norwegian People's Peace Prize went into the Peace People Trust, to our headquarters, "Fredheim," the Peace House on Lisburn Road in Belfast, and to loans and grants to any community or cooperative project which served the aims of the declaration.

⚭

The first half of 1976 was the worst single period of sectarian murders during the entire Troubles, but the second half of 1976 saw the biggest single drop in violence during that same period. The Peace People movement continued to work for reconciliation and justice. Perhaps the most important justice issue was the prison situation, and we began to address that situation, which caused great controversy and strain within our movement.

Perhaps we were trying to do too much. Perhaps we put so much energy into our peace work that we lost sight of our relationships. Perhaps we also lost sight of the fact that people are more important than projects. Perhaps we were so busy trying to solve all the problems outside that we did not take enough time to meditate and pray for our own inner peace.

For whatever reasons, by the winter of 1980, the Peace People movement had become "unpeaceful" and the trust which had made it possible to hold together so many people from so many different backgrounds and viewpoints had gone. There is no doubt that if people trust each other, they can do anything, but once the trust goes, everything becomes impossible.

⚬⚭⚬

After our movement split, we made a conscious decision to put the past behind us and to get on with the work with strong determination. Our October 1980 assembly was one of the best, with a platform of speakers from across the political spectrum and with participation from those previously associated with paramilitaries. This occurred during a time when it was hard to get people to talk at all and when the threat of the prison hunger strike hung over us.

Throughout these years, we have carried on the work of peacemaking with that same determination. We continue to form peace groups, advocate welfare reform, demand justice, especially for prisoners, call for the repeal of the emergency laws, encourage young people to become peacemakers, publish our newspaper, hold youth camps, and support other international peace campaigns. The fact that so many have persisted in this work and that new, younger members continue to join us is a source of hope and inspiration for me.

However important our programs are, it is the spirit underlying the work that is most important. The way in which we walk together toward our shared vision of a peaceful world shapes the coming of that peace. In the past we allowed the spirit of the movement to die. If we do not learn from our past mistakes and go forward determined to avoid making those mistakes again, we will waste our time looking back. For me, peacemaking is hard, it is painful, but it is teaching me lessons for the future.

I have learned that love enables us to transcend all differences. I have learned that if we speak the truth in love and stand by that truth no matter what the cost, it will lead us to trust one another. I have learned that when people trust each other, they can work together on many critical issues, no matter how differently they may feel about them. I have learned that if we are to benefit from our history, we have to be able to talk about it all, to each other, without anger and without fear. I have learned too that personal relationships are important, that we must make time for each other, time to listen, to be sensitive, to forgive, and to show compassion toward each other.

Above all, I have learned that we need to aim at inner peace through regular prayer and meditation. We can join with others to pray for an end to the violence. It is important to recognize that we are all guilty of violence in thought, word, and action toward each other, and that we must say that we are sorry for the hurt we have caused each other.

And so, as we rededicate ourselves to peacemaking, let us thank God for allowing us to learn from our mistakes and for helping us to persevere in our work and for the good work God has helped us to do. But above all, let us thank God for the gift of each other and the joy we experience in our friendships as we walk together on the path to peace.

2

The Way Forward
for Northern Ireland

Northern Ireland is a microcosm of the world. In Northern Ireland we have diseased relationships. We have two cultures that have never learned to live together as brothers and sisters under proper political and just structures, without hate, without guns, and without killing. Look around the world today and you'll find even on your own doorstep that humanity has not yet learned to deal with these problems. As we reflect about the question of Northern Ireland, the question for us is: "How do we learn from our mistakes so that we do not repeat them?"

The community in which I grew up and live is called Andersonstown, which is a continuation of the Falls Road, the Catholic section of Belfast. Up until the late 1960s, in that huge community we had no local police station. Some of us thought we should have police stations in case the law was broken. When we asked for one, they replied, "You do not need a police station. Young people do not break the law here. You are highly disciplined." You could say even now in Northern Ireland that we are a highly disciplined people.

A few weeks ago, I spoke to a young nun who works in a prison not far from Andersonstown.

"Why are you so interested in prison work, Sister?" I asked.

"When I was asked to do parish work and I knocked on the neighborhood doors," she replied, "I discovered at every other home there was a young man either imprisoned or emigrated or on the run or on remand. I decided my work was in the prisons where so many of our young men are."

Up until the 1960s, we had practically no prison population. Now we have the youngest prison population in Western Europe. Two-thirds of our men now in prison were under the age of fifteen when the Troubles started in the North. One-third were seven years of age when the Troubles started. Why has our society found itself in this situation?

Transcribed text of a speech given without notes at St. Michael's College, Vermont, November 1981.

When the civil rights movement began in Northern Ireland in the late 1960s, it was a nonviolent movement that rose from the example of Martin Luther King, Jr. We were asking for basic human rights in Northern Ireland, for equal employment opportunities, better housing, and a vote for everyone. Unfortunately, the civil rights movement didn't get those reforms quickly enough from the government. Despite the wishes of the more liberal members of the movement, a march was planned from Belfast to Derry in 1969. This march was attacked at Burntolet Bridge by loyalists and hence gave support to militant republicans' argument that nothing could be achieved without violence. In the past Northern militant republicans had used violence without any popular support. This mass movement for civil rights was used instead. The collapse of the civil rights movement led to street violence conducted by militants on both sides, resulting in many people being burned out of their homes as the sectarian demons were released. Out of this, the provisional Irish Republican Army was born and so also was the Ulster Loyal Paramilitaries.

Would we have found ourselves in that situation if we had a police force which acted responsibly? History might have been different if they had acted responsibly. But they did not. We had a police force acting out of fear which opened fire on the community, killing, beating, and imprisoning many people. They were no longer respected within the Catholic community, and the British army was brought on to our streets at the request of the Catholics in late 1969.

Whatever you think about armies, in the end all armies are trained to kill. That's why we have them. The British army was brought into Northern Ireland in 1969 onto the Falls Road and other Catholic areas in Belfast and elsewhere to do what was primarily a community policing job. But that wasn't what they were trained to do. After a very short period, we experienced a complete reversal. The army, which had been treated to tea in every Catholic community, was now feared by the same community. The army began searching and destroying thousands of homes in an attempt to find any IRA unit beginning to form. But the IRA was not active in 1969.

I come from that area, and in 1969 the IRA did not exist there. But soon afterward, the British introduced internment and the IRA made its greatest recruiting drive there among the Catholic population. When internment began, over three hundred men were dragged out of their beds in the middle of the night and put into makeshift prisons with absolutely no recourse to the law. The community in Northern Ireland, particularly the Catholic community, was so angered, that the IRA began to get many recruits. Later, thank God, internment was phased out.

But then the emergency laws were implemented. Under this state of emergency, juries were set aside for single-judge courts. This means that people can be convicted because of signed confessions. The Emergency Provisions Act gives the army and the police very wide powers of arrest and detention, and it creates a sense of bitterness and indignity among the population. When the emergency laws began to be implemented, more and more of our people were sent to prisons. The IRA became more active, killing people regularly. The UDA, the Protestant paramilitary formed to protect the community, took up guns and started killing and destroying the communities.

We quickly found ourselves caught between the British army and the paramilitary groups, the IRA and the Loyalist Volunteer Force. Every day on the streets of Northern Ireland there was bloodshed and death with no end to the cycle of violence.

Nonetheless, the vast majority of the people of Northern Ireland want nothing to do with violence.

It was a miracle when the Peace People movement started in 1976, because at that stage we genuinely believed that we were on the brink of civil war. We were looking to our churches for leadership. We were looking to our politicians for leadership. And we never received any. People didn't know what to do. Everyone was afraid. But when the peace movement started organizing marches for peace all around the North, after the death of my sister's three little children — the price of war — people mobilized in the thousands to try to stop the war and build a more peaceful, more just society.

It is incredible that humanity knows how to make war and how to build up armaments and guns, and yet we know nothing about how to make peace. We are only babes when it comes to peacemaking. We know so little about the effective tools of nonviolence. That was and remains our problem today.

In August 1976, we rallied thousands of people in the streets who said No! to the violence. But then we needed a strategy to build proper community politics and structures. Perhaps if we had more information, it might have worked. People responded to the call for peace. Many ex-paramilitaries joined the call for peace. The loyalist paramilitary group, the UDA, after one year, put up the gun and started talking about an independent Northern Ireland and called a cease-fire. The IRA refused to talk. Our strategy was that we needed everybody to talk. We don't want to bury the IRA. We know how they came into existence. They emerged from our community, and we knew some of them very well. We were trying to bring them into the community to talk about a political way forward for our country. But they refused to move.

The government had the opportunity then to make the necessary changes for peace, but they refused to move, too. In the peace movement, we understood very quickly that peace comes through justice, and so we began to address the injustices in the North. We lost many members because many people would prefer to pray to God and hope the problems go away. They do not see the genuine, structural inhumanities present in our society. Perhaps this is where Christianity has failed most. We Christians rarely recognize the suffering Christ present in those who do not have a house or a decent job or proper political structures or basic human dignity.

At that stage, we began to examine the emergency laws and to lobby at Westminster to ask the government to return us to fair, just laws. We proved statistically that the implementation of the emergency laws destroys respect for law and order. We know that in Northern Ireland today. People ask, "Why should I have respect for the law when the law has no respect for me?" The answer to terrorism is not the implementation of legalized terrorism on a greater scale. The answer is not the removal of a fair judicial system. But that is precisely the unjust situation in Northern Ireland today.

We began to study the prison situation because we know that until the prison issue is solved, there will be no political development in the North. In 1976, the British government removed political status for prisoners. In 1977, we looked at the prison conditions and we pleaded with the government to give the prisoners at least the fair recognition of emergency status, since they are emergency prisoners convicted under the emergency laws. We demanded widespread prison reform. But the government refused to listen. Why do societies dehumanize people in prison? Why do we humiliate them? Why do we punish them even more?

These are the questions we have been asking. We have young men coming to the Peace People movement. "I'm only just out of prison," they say. "I can't go back into the Catholic community," some say, "because the IRA wants me to become an active member again." Others say, "I can't go back into the Protestant community because the loyalists want me to become active again. Can you help me get a job?" And we can't get them jobs. They have no hope. We have hundreds of them beginning to come back out with nothing to offer them. What is it about this society? Why are we so insane about punishing people over and over again? Where is Christian compassion? Where is the understanding? How can we solve these crises?

Sadly, in the North of Ireland, many so-called Christians have been calling for a return to hanging or shooting prisoners. Those people who shout the loudest are the most powerful. Even today, you can turn on your television set in Belfast and you can see that the so-called leaders who call for renewed hate and anger and killing are walking the streets of Belfast. They are not the ones who die. They are not the ones who get locked up in prison. It is always some teenager, sixteen or seventeen years old, from the ghetto who takes the gun and does the dirty work and ends up in prison.

Who is guilty and who is innocent? In Northern Ireland, no one is without blame. We have sat back for so long and allowed these injustices to grow like a cancer in our society. We have said our prayers and said nothing so that we would not get into any trouble. We are all guilty.

The prison issue, like all these justice issues, is far from solved. We hope, please God, it will be someday soon. To us, the greatest sorrow was the death of ten hunger strikers and the fact that there was three times the violence and killing in our community during the hunger strike. Do you remember the name of any of the young policemen who were murdered by the IRA while the hunger strikers were dying? They are our brothers as much as Bobby Sands dying in prison is our brother.

We have such deep problems within the system, such unjust structures, and we do our best to address them. We are a divided community in Northern Ireland. We are polarized. We go to separate Catholic schools. We live in separate Catholic communities. You can grow up to be sixteen in Northern Ireland and never meet a Protestant. If you're lucky, you may live in one of the more middle-class areas which are slightly mixed. Our dream is that we will move toward a greater number of mixed communities.

But as a movement, we are committed to justice and peace, even if we lose all our members. We believe we have to talk about the issues which must be solved before we can move forward. People talk about a simple answer, and it would be easy for me to stand here and claim there is a simple answer and win your affections by saying we'll unite our island and get the British out. I can't give you a simple answer. All I can say is that if you have a house and two people are fighting in it, you don't buy the house next door, knock the wall down, and extend the fighting area. You try to solve the problem in the house first, and then you move forward from there.

In Northern Ireland, we have only one and a half million people. God love them, they're the best in the world. If you ever come, you'll fall in love with us and you'll not even want to return home. But we have our problems. When it comes to the political issues, when it comes to the fear between the communities, when it comes to holding on to what little one has, unfortunately, we fight. Still, many of us are working for peace.

But perhaps the most exciting development in the North of Ireland, and around the world, is that at this stage in history, many of us are realizing that the way forward is no longer the old way of taking up the gun, fighting a revolutionary cause with a bomb, or fighting over political issues with bullets. Violence has created only further violence and hatred and broken hearts. In Northern Ireland, we can prove it.

Northern Ireland is full of family members of the dead, wives of young policemen, the families of the hunger strikers, and in England, the wives of young soldiers. Our hospitals are full of men in wheelchairs, half-blind, without arms, permanently wounded. People are beginning to realize that there's got to be another way to solve our problems. The price of war is too high. The whole idea of war, the so-called just war theory, the notion that Christians can arms themselves and kill their enemies and still follow Christ, has come into question in Ireland.

I remember once visiting a Catholic school in Derry and saying to a fourteen-year-old boy, "Don't stay in the IRA. Get out of it." And he said, "Oh, no, I'm in the IRA to kill for the cause. I believe in the cause!"

That kid didn't know what a just war was. Somebody told him something like that, and so he is fighting for a just war. The day the churches blessed war, they denied Christ, because Christ told us to love our enemies and not to be afraid. He died on a cross. He refused to support killing. He lived in an occupied country. He didn't join the oppressive forces or the revolutionary forces. He spoke about love. No matter how much we try to argue for violence, when you come back to it, you can't get past the fact that Christ was a pacifist. I can't get beyond that.

Wherever we are, wherever we live, we need to ask ourselves as Christians, if Christ lived in Belfast, would he carry a gun and kill others for the cause? If Christ lived in America would he prepare for, maintain, or support nuclear weapons, a limited nuclear war that could annihilate millions of our sisters and brothers in the world? That's your question. I have answered it for myself, and my answer is, No, he wouldn't.

What's exciting is that back home many people are beginning to declare, "We are a people of peace." We can go back to the core message of Christianity and live Christ's way of peace. We are sisters and brothers living in a world where so many hungry people are crying out to be fed, where the best minds are planning mass destruction instead of feeding the starving. There is something deadly wrong in our world today. In Belfast we struggle, and it's a daily struggle for justice and peace, but we do it with joy. It is a privilege to be working for justice and peace and for a new way forward for Ireland and the North.

I hope you will join us in that struggle. You don't need to be with us on the streets of Belfast. There is much to be done for human rights, for peace, for reconciliation and justice right where you are. Together we can say, "We are a people of peace." This is the way forward for the world.

We cannot go back. Neither can we stand still. But we can go forward together in a spirit of solidarity with a new vision of peace for Northern Ireland and for our world.

3

A New Vision, A Fresh Wisdom

On the evening of August 14, 1969, the word was all around Andersonstown that people on the Lower Falls Road in Belfast were being burned out of their homes by "loyalist extremists." I drove down to see if my Aunt Maggie was all right.

I stood in the middle of Norfolk Street (where she had lived all her life) watching a scene of confusion and terror. Houses were being torched by loyalists, police stood by watching, and Catholics ran about frantically trying to salvage what they could from their burning homes.

Furniture was lowered from upper windows. Some fell smashing into pieces on the footpaths below. A Sacred Heart picture was lowered on a rope from an upper window, and the glass broke as it hit the ground. People loaded bits of furniture into cars, old vans, anything that moved. I helped some people get out what few possessions they could.

Of the many memories of that dreadful evening, one picture stands out in my mind. In the midst of the terror, I saw a beautiful china cabinet standing right in the middle of Norfolk Street, with people running all around it. It was in perfect condition and looked very beautiful. I thought, "It'll be a miracle if that china cabinet survives."

Aunt Maggie was eventually rehoused on one of the top floors of Divis flats, the tall apartment buildings at the entrance of the Falls Road. She never liked it. Once she said to me, "I'm buried above ground waiting to be buried below." She missed her friends and she missed Norfolk Street. Norfolk Street is not there anymore.

A short time later I visited some families in their prefabricated huts. These huts had been put up hastily in the heart of Andersonstown to house some of the hundreds of families who had been burnt out or had fled in terror. To my amazement, I saw in one of the huts the china cabinet. Its owner told me how not so much as a cup had been broken, and she opened it to show me the family photos which had been saved.

Published in the *Belfast Telegraph,* August 15, 1994.

In a nearby hut, a young mother wept as she told me how damp and cold the huts were, and how her young baby girl had just died of pneumonia. The china cabinet was saved. A precious little life was not. She was not even a Troubles statistic. Little did I imagine that there would be over thirty-two hundred more deaths in the long, cruel war then erupting.

Last week, I spent an evening walking through some of the streets on the Lower Falls. I was with a group of Peace People selling our newspaper, *Peace by Peace*. In Bombay Street, which was almost entirely burned out in 1969, some things have changed, but much remains the same. A local youth club leader said this was a small, close-knit community where memories are long. People continue to suffer and the peace process would be "a long, hard process." He said he didn't agree with violence, but neither did he support the Downing Street Declaration (the recent agreement between Britain and Ireland).

A group of teenagers played ball beside the giant wall which divides the Catholic and Protestant neighborhoods in Belfast. They were friendly. One recalled her granny walking in the Peace People rallies. They asked if we were having any more rallies. Yes, they said, they wanted peace. We asked if they were interested in starting a peace group in their area. One girl quipped, "Do the Peace People pay the hospital bills?" They are afraid of the IRA, and in an area where the IRA has exiled, kneecapped, or executed local people, it is understandable that most people prefer to keep their heads down.

A few weeks earlier, when I was visiting the same area, some residents had to remove iron bars used to block their own front doors. I was told that the bars keep "the enemy" out. Tragically, the greatest enemy in this community and on the other side of the wall is fear. And this enemy is already within. People are deeply afraid. But as the saying goes, there is nothing to fear but fear itself.

All during our visit, a helicopter hovered in the air above us. It made a terrible drone, but when I remarked about the awful noise, people just shrugged their shoulders. An early Peace People marcher, Josie, brought me in for coffee. When I mentioned the helicopter noise, she said with an air of resignation, "We get it when there's trouble on the Shankill Road (in the Protestant section). We get it when there's trouble on the Falls

Road (in the Catholic section). And we get it when there's no trouble."

Farther down the next street, three military vehicles pulled up. Eight policemen got out, followed by four soldiers. The rest remained inside. Two policemen went to the door of a house, while the soldiers, who looked no more than eighteen years old, took up positions at the corners, cocking their machine guns in various directions. A few neighbors came out to watch. It was calm. There was no panic. The children played on. No stones were thrown, no bin lids banged on the ground. No answer at the door. The security forces returned to their vehicles and drove away. No one opened their door to us down the rest of the street.

I watched this scene with mixed emotions. I kept thinking people shouldn't have to live like this. How would I feel if my son or daughter was put into the back of one of these dark, gray military vehicles and taken to Castlereagh police interrogation center under the emergency provisions, provisions under which some men have signed confessions for crimes they did not commit, because of the torture or threats they suffered.

It's all very well to talk about not giving into fear and having courage, but when we know people are open to abuse under this emergency legislation, then we may expect very natural feelings of fear and anger to come to the surface. The British government's emergency laws are immoral and counterproductive and must be repealed immediately.

These unjust laws lead young men to join the paramilitaries because they are angered by the action of the security forces in their communities. It is a tragedy and a truth that many years after the civil rights movement, the quality of justice is lower than ever in Northern Ireland. These laws are a block to real peace. Their progressive repeal will be part of a real peace process.

The IRA and their loyalist equivalents must take responsibility for the prolonging of this oppressive injustice, over and above their part in bringing fear, suffering, and death to their fellow human beings in their own communities and far beyond them.

Members of the republican movement believe in freedom. Today they must ask themselves what they mean by this word. Is there not something badly wrong with the methods they are

using when many people in their own communities are afraid
of them?

Today in Ireland the "armed struggle" is destroying the very
freedom of the very people in whose name it is pursued. The
"armed struggle" is going nowhere, except a cul-de-sac of fear,
division, death, and destruction.

It is time for a nonviolent alternative. Some argue that nonviolence doesn't work, as if that proved that violence does
work. "I use nonviolence not because it works but because it
is right," Gandhi wrote as he led a revolution against British
imperialism. For people who need confidence in order to face
their fear, it is important to understand that while nonviolence
takes time, it does work.

Nonviolence above all never takes human life. It upholds the
sanctity and right to life and dignity of every human being. It
is crazy, as well as cruel, to take human life in an attempt to
build a new and better society that upholds human life. I do not
doubt the courage, energy, commitment and love of many who
have engaged in the "armed struggle" on one side or another.
They have paid and continue to pay a high price and will want
to remain faithful to their sacrifice. I do believe though that
now is the time to allow wisdom and perception to open our
hearts and minds to a wider perspective on the reality of today's
Ireland, North and South.

Much has changed. Many people in Northern Ireland, and
not only unionists, do not want their future determined by
people in the South of Ireland, any more than would people
in the Republic want Northern Ireland to dictate its future.

The Republic and Britain have already "self-determined"
their own futures. Seventy years into partition the two parts of
Ireland have diverged to such an extent that we now need two
separate jurisdictions, one for the Republic, one for Northern
Ireland. Put to the test, most people in the Republic do not
want Irish unity. Ninety percent have never spent a night in
Northern Ireland. Britain too would be happy to part with us if
they could see an honorable way out.

The truth is that the Northern Irish people have really only
got each other. Together, we can build a Northern Irish political identity and replace old-style majority rule and tribal party
politics with a system of politics based on local communities,
establishing genuine democracy from the bottom up. We are

all challenged to begin to think in a completely new way about our relationships, our political institutions. A new vision and a fresh wisdom can be brought to birth, but only after each of us, however painfully, has reexamined much of our current thinking. We can build on the grounds of new realities and clearer perspectives of how things are now. Then we can move forward together.

Radical new thinking and solutions to our "troubles" will not be imposed from on high by the British or Irish governments. It will come, as it must come, sooner or later, out of communities themselves, such as Clonard, Shankill, East Belfast, Markets, and all the other urban and rural villages which make up the Northern Irish community.

From these highly politicized, imaginative, patient people will come a new vision and hope for us all. It will come. The only real question is how soon will this real peace process break through to replace, once and for all, the violent division of a people who do not wish to be violent and who long for peace.

The timing of that day is up to every one of us. It will be delayed as long as we sit back and let divisions continue to be expressed politically and paramilitarily. It will come sooner if we translate our longing into action, and each one of us plays our part. Too many have been buried above and below the ground. It is time to begin again the quest for peace in Northern Ireland.

4

The Death of My Sister

Today is the seventh anniversary of the death of my sister Anne Maguire.

On January 21, 1980, at around 3:00 p.m., Anne took her own life, and her spirit found peace at last.

Her husband, Jackie, a motor mechanic in a local firm, was at work. One of her daughters, Joanne (two and a half), was at nursery school, and baby Marie-Louise (nine months old) lay upstairs in her cot. Her ten-year-old son, Mark, returned from school to find his mother sitting in a chair, dying or dead from her wounds. Anne had taken an electric knife and cut her wrists. We were told it would have taken about thirty minutes for Anne to "bleed to death." Before dying, she took the kitchen mop and tried to clean up her blood from the floor. An unfinished note to her family lay beside her. It read, "Forgive me. I love you."

Anne was buried in Milltown Cemetery, alongside her three other little children, who had been killed in August 1976. She herself had chosen the words on their gravestone: "They died so others might live in peace." In a way Anne had really died then, too, only her poor, bruised, broken body had lingered on, longing for the day when she too could join them in heaven.

Joanne (eight), John (two and a half), and Andrew (six weeks) had been killed on August 10, 1976, in a clash between an IRA active service unit and a British army patrol on Finaghy Road North, Belfast. Danny Lennon, a nineteen-year-old IRA man, was shot through the head by a British soldier. His car swerved onto the footpath killing three of Anne's children (only Mark was saved) and injuring Anne herself.

Anne was unconscious for almost two weeks, dangerously ill, and not expected to live. She did survive. Her broken legs and pelvis required many months of slowly learning to walk again. One of her first outings was to the Falls Road rally where she stood before thousands of people and read the Declaration

Published in the *Belfast Telegraph,* January 21, 1997.

of the Peace People. She also went to visit Mrs. Lennon, for as she said, "She has lost her child, too."

Anne never saw her children buried. In her own mind she refused to accept their deaths. She would often talk about seeing them playing in the garden. Their deaths and the brain bruising she suffered resulted in psychotic depression. Anne became a troubled soul, knowing no peace of mind.

In the spring of 1977, Jackie, Anne, and Mark Maguire emigrated to New Zealand. There a daughter, Joanne, was born to them. But even this great joy was overshadowed by the memory of the children who died. She made garlands for them out of the flowers sent by our family. She seemed to lock herself in a private world with her dead babies. Jackie decided to bring his family back home.

In April 1979, in Belfast, a second daughter, Marie-Louise, was born. We all rejoiced, and for a short while fooled ourselves into thinking that Anne was getting better. However, as we all know, death anniversaries can be powerful forces and the tenth of August found Anne reliving the cruel nightmare of past days. She tried several times to end it all, and in desperation Jackie turned everywhere for help. Anne seemed beyond the help of modern medicine. We were told that, as she was a "determined suicide," we could only pray and watch out for her.

Finally, in a painful, slow, lonely death, on a bitter cold winter's day, Anne's spirit flew away to join her little angels in heaven. She was thirty-one years old when her agony started, and thirty-five when it ended.

The family gathers together each year for a Mass on the anniversary. We remember Anne, and how she used to laugh and sing. We laugh and sing now and are very happy, as she would want us to be. But it took many years for each of us to learn to surrender the past and celebrate the present. And we continue to struggle with this challenge. For many of us, deep down, we cry for Anne and wish it had not been her and her three little children on Finaghy Road North on August 10, 1976. We also wish the IRA and the British army had not been there, so that Anne and the children could have gone to the library as they planned that day, visited Granny, and walked home to make dinner for Jackie when he returned from work. But it was not to be so.

Why, some people will ask, am I only now telling Anne's story? Because she is not here to tell it herself. She never lived to write of the violence that she suffered in her own short life. I am telling it also on behalf of the thousands of people who have suffered through twenty-seven years of the Troubles. I am telling it because violence and war are wrong.

I believe her story needs to be told to remind us all to struggle in a nonviolent way to build a just and peaceful society and to have the courage to help those who use violent ways to see that it is wrong to kill no matter how just they might feel their cause to be. It is incumbent upon our generation to affirm that violence is against our oldest Christian tradition. In the fifth century, St. Patrick told those who would resort to violence: "Killing cannot be with Christ." We need to hear these words of St. Patrick again.

Isn't it time for the IRA to cease their violence and start talking in earnest? Isn't it time too for the INLA (the Irish National Liberation Army, a paramilitary organization) and the loyalist paramilitaries to end their threat of violence? In Anne's name, and in the name of all who have suffered, I appeal to the IRA: "Give us a cease-fire and we will move heaven and earth to get inclusive talks immediately." Around the world the use of violence for political ends is becoming a thing of the past. Surely the republican movement does not want to condemn us all to live in the past?

Once a cease-fire is in place, there will be no valid excuse for unionist politicians not to talk with Sinn Fein. If they do not talk, how are they to solve the problem?

I have told the story of Anne not to make anyone sad, but to give everyone hope. The story of Anne will be told long after all of us have gone to be with her. But let those who remember her story speak of her compassion, her courage, her joy, and above all her love for her family. We don't believe that Anne has gone from us. We see her and feel her presence with us all the time.

I am certain that her wish for us all is simple and clear: End the violence forever and live in peace.

5

An Open Letter to the IRA

A chara, Dear Brothers and Sisters,

You will have often noticed how salty are the tears that roll down into your mouth. I often experience this, especially when I sit in the little Chapel of Adoration on the Falls Road in Belfast, where I am now writing this letter. I find myself today experiencing here even more deeply the pain of the people of this community, and I weep at the pity of it all. I was born a short distance away and went to school around the corner in St. Vincent's. This is home. This is where I come from. I love this place. More than that, I love the people of this community.

Some will say, "You moved away. You live in the country now." I do. But suffering from a distance heightens the pain of separation and solitude. Thankfully, the pain has eased, and often turns to joy when I talk to the people living along this road. They have a deep faith, a faith which leads to hope and perseverance. They know all will be well. For many years they have prayed for peace, as have many others in Northern Ireland.

Here, though, the desire for peace is passionate, tangible. You feel you could reach out and touch it. Without their having to explain it to you, you know that the people here have a deep sense of what peace is, and what peace is not — something born in them out of a long history of never knowing real peace.

The question they always ask me, but now even more so, is whether there will be genuine peace. I sense in this community an excited anticipation that the time is now, and that the opportunity for a genuine peace has never been greater. The people want this creative peace. They yearn for it, they cry out, they pray for it, with an earnestness that inspires and energizes me.

There have been other times before, just as intense, when people have cried out for peace. In 1976 during the Peace People rallies, more than half a million people from North and South walked for peace. This movement began when my sister Anne and her husband, Jackie's, three children, Joanne (eight),

---

Published in the *Irish News,* December 1993.

John (almost three), and Andrew (six-weeks old) were killed in a clash between the British army and the IRA.

On the day the three children were buried, August 14, 1976, I took roses off their grave and brought them to Mrs. Lennon. She was the mother of Danny Lennon, your young comrade who had been shot through the head by a soldier and whose car had swerved off the road killing the three children and injuring Anne. I mourned for young Danny Lennon and shared the grief of his family. I hoped and prayed at that time that his death and the deaths of my niece and nephews would be the end of all violent deaths in our country. They were not.

In the past twenty-five years, more than thirty-two hundred people have been killed, leaving behind unimaginable suffering and pain for their families. You and your comrades in the IRA take responsibility for your part in causing this bloodshed. All of you in your time will want to say "Sorry." And so will others who for their reasons have inflicted so much pain on their fellow human beings here.

You and your comrades are not strangers to suffering. In the days ahead as you choose between the peace framework or the "armed struggle," Bobby Sands and many others who have died will be in your thoughts. You will want to remain faithful to their sacrifice for a free and united Ireland. That's only human. But change is also part of being human. As John Henry Newman says, "In a higher world, it is otherwise, but here below, to live is to change, and to be perfect is to have changed often."

In the republican movement, you are now faced with the need to change radically, to move away from the "armed struggle" and into a nonviolent alternative. Your right to your political aspiration and national identity has been acknowledged. The way of active nonviolence is in tune with your Christian roots and heritage. You know that in your heart. As a child, you learned to pray, "Help me to live like Jesus." Jesus with a machine gun does not come off as an authentic figure! It is time now for a new vision and a fresh wisdom.

Wisdom means the tough decision to walk the path of nonviolence. That risk of faith will take all your courage. No one doubts your courage and no one doubts your ability to carry on the "armed struggle." However, I doubt your ability to turn a deaf ear to the cries of people for peace now. I know that you have a love for people in your heart and I pray that your heart and their hearts may be as one.

A new vision and a fresh wisdom are not only necessary for the republican movement, they are necessary for the future of humanity. Each of us personally has to search our own hearts to find these treasures. In my own journey, I have come to know for certain that every human life is sacred and a gift. We have no right to take this gift of life from another, as they have no right to take our gift.

I have come to know for certain that our first identity is not nationalist or unionist, but our shared humanity. I have come to know for certain that love and compassion are the greatest and strongest forces operating in our world today.

I believe and work for a nonviolent, demilitarized, Northern Irish society, and I hope our friends in the South of Ireland will begin also to work for a demilitarized, nonviolent Ireland. Then we will truly be a "light" in a highly militarized world. Our suffering will then have been the birth pangs of a truly civilized people living together as the community of God's beloved people.

I sith agus I muinteras Iosa, in the peace and in the company of Jesus,

Siochain, Shalom, Peace,
Mairead

6

There Is No Just War:
A Letter to Gerry Adams

You are completely right when you say the Catholic Church is not a pacifist church. But is this not a defect in our church teaching? Is not this one more case in which we are unfaithful to the gospel of Jesus Christ?

The church may not be pacifist, but Jesus is a pacifist, and our early Christian roots are indeed pacifist. As Fr. John Mc-Kenzie, theologian and biblical scholar, writes, "If we cannot know from the New Testament that Jesus rejected violence absolutely, then we can know nothing of Jesus' person or message. It is the clearest of themes."

As "Christ"-ians, we are called to be "Christ"-like. We are called to struggle, joyfully and painfully, to live our lives based on nonviolence and a love for our enemies according to the life of Jesus.

The individual Christian cannot refuse to live out Jesus' message of nonviolence and love of enemies simply because the mainline churches, for seventeen hundred years, have not believed, taught, or lived his simple message, "No more killing."

For the first three hundred years after Christ, the early Christian communities lived a total commitment to Jesus' way of nonviolence. In 215 C.E. Hippolytus wrote: "The soldier [who becomes a Christian] shall not kill anyone. If ordered to do so, he shall not carry out the order. If he does not accept this, let him be dismissed [from the Christian community]. The catechumen or believer who wishes to become a soldier shall be dismissed [from the Christian community]."

Sadly, during the last seventeen hundred years, Christians have moved so far away from the Christic life of nonviolence that we find ourselves in the terrible dilemma of condemning one kind of homicide and violence while paying for, actively

Published in the *Irish News,* June 18, 1990, in response to an article by Sinn Fein president Gerry Adams, defending the use of violence, published the week before.

participating in, or supporting homicide, violence, and war on a magnitude far greater than what we condemn in others.

In this, you are correct. You point to a longstanding defect in our theology. To help us out of this dilemma, we need to hear the full gospel message from our Christian leaders. We need to develop a theology of nonviolence. It is not enough to talk about community relations and peacemaking, however valuable this may be. This is not what Jesus talked about.

Some people in Ireland, particularly our youth, believe in good faith that the "just war theory" can be applied to "the Irish problem." In their attempt to find justice, they have turned to "the armed struggle." The church leadership and our traditional theology must bear part of the responsibility for this situation. It is not up to us to condemn our sisters and brothers who have taken this misguided path to justice. We owe it to ourselves and them to admit our part in their decision.

What is needed in Ireland — and the Christian world — is for all church leaders and Christians to renounce the lie of the just war theory. Fr. John McKenzie describes the just war theory as "a phony piece of morality." And that is why we need a new theology of nonviolence and peace.

No war has ever been fought based on the theoretic principles outlining a so-called "just war." Take, for example, one of the conditions: "useless violence and carnage should be avoided." When so-called Christian Americans dropped the atomic bombs on Hiroshima and Nagasaki, no one consulted the just war principles. What is needed in Ireland — and the world today — is the unambiguous proclamation that violence is a lie, that violence is not the way of Jesus, and that violence is not the way of Christians. The Christian message is simple: "Tell people to stop killing each other and to start loving one another, including their enemies." It is simply not being said.

This will not be easy, but with God's grace it is possible. It means admitting that for seventeen hundred years Christians have not lived the full gospel message. Here in Ireland, it means facing some hard truths. It must be said clearly by church leaders, and by all Christians, that if today "the armed struggle" is not the Christian way, then "the armed struggle" of 1916–22 was not the Christian way. If the vicious circle is to be broken in Ireland and a new generation is to be prevented from carrying on "the armed struggle," then this truth must be spoken clearly.

Must not nonviolence be offered as the only option open to those Christians who wish to carry on their legitimate political aspirations? Christian leadership must bear some part of the responsibility for the decision taken by those who chose violence to further their political aims. If Jesus' nonviolence is not being taught in our seminaries and has never been taught, if our educators have not been taught about nonviolence, then how can people make informed choices between allegedly justified violence or Jesus' nonviolence? How can we expect people to choose nonviolence?

"If the church is not commissioned to teach what Jesus taught," Fr. Charles McCarthy asks, "then what is she commissioned to teach?" If there is to be any hope for Christianity and humanity's survival, must not nonviolence be taught at every level of society?

You ask for suggested strategies. If we choose to be Christian before being nationalistic or materialistic, then the question before us is: "What strategy would Christ use?" Fr. McKenzie points out what Christ wouldn't use: "All the gospels agree that Jesus refused armed defense." "One rejects violence whether it is committed by the oppressor or the oppressed, and no theological education is needed to see that Jesus with a machine gun is not an authentic figure. Jesus taught us much about how to die. He taught and showed us nothing about how to kill."

Jesus' strategy is "love your neighbor as yourself" and "love your enemies." This means we overcome evil through active nonviolence. We respect the humanity of each person, even if we cannot agree with that person's actions. Our strategy is dialogue. It is a necessary first step. It is up to every one to make dialogue possible. We all need to recognize the possibility that we ourselves can change, and our neighbor can change also.

We are all responsible for the terrible situation of pain and suffering here in the North. We must all ask forgiveness and move forward through dialogue, respect, and trust of one another. I can only ask you not to get discouraged in your quest for dialogue with others.

You wrote in your article that "my receiving the Eucharist or not is none of your business." I agree. The Scriptures tell us whose business it is: the individual, those who have something against him and God. In chapter five of Matthew, verse 23, we read, "So if you are standing before the altar in the temple, offering a sacrifice to God, and suddenly remember that a friend has something against you, leave your sacrifice there beside the altar and go and apologize and be reconciled to him, and then come and offer your sacrifice to God."

In a community as deeply divided as ours, shouldn't every Christian take the initiative and move forward toward reconciliation? Christ has called us to take that step.

Shalom,
Mairead

7

The Politics of Mercy and Forgiveness

On the morning after the former loyalist paramilitary Bobby Bates was shot, the Peace People arranged a small prayer service at the spot where he was murdered. His wife, Carol, his mother and father, his sister Margaret, and his friends and co-workers came to mourn his death. Young people whom Bobby had helped came to lay flowers and remember his kindness to them. Bobby's friend and co-worker, Martin Snoddin, led the proceedings. Three Protestant ministers and a Catholic priest led the group in prayer and thanked God for his mercy and forgiveness to Bobby and us all.

Like all of us, Bobby Bates was in need of God's mercy. As a loyalist paramilitary, active in the mid-1970s in Belfast, he took the lives of many people. We must never forget the pain and loss their relatives and friends carry with them.

But Bobby Bates was also a victim. I once heard an ex-prisoner say that when he was locked into his prison cell each night, he was never alone. He was locked up with the memory of the person he had murdered. He could never escape from him. Bobby Bates was locked up in prison for twenty years with those memories. In that time, he often relived the horror of his crimes of cruelty and murder. One day in prison, the full realization of what he had done came upon him. Mercifully, by the grace of God, he repented, asked forgiveness, and showed great remorse for what he had done.

When he was released from prison, he began to work with young people in his community. He would walk with young Protestant boys through his neighborhood and point out the murals along the walls which depict armed gunmen in action. He implored the boys not to get involved with the loyalist paramilitaries. Instead, he urged them to get an education, take up sports, and work for peace and reconciliation.

Published in *The Citizen* (the Peace People newspaper) December 1997.

This was a risky message to be preaching in the face of the militants arguing for a return to all-out violence and war. It called for great courage on his part. Bobby knew the risks he was taking, but he continued to work for peace, believing that education was the key to steering young people away from sectarianism. He had learned that peaceful means, not violence, was the way forward for us all. It took courage for him to go into other communities and across the political and religious divide and to speak out for peace. But he did it. Once he met a group of Swedish peace activists visiting the Peace People headquarters and spoke out against violence. The visitors were moved and inspired by his presence and message.

Two weeks later he was murdered.

Bobby spent much of his time working for ex-prisoners and their families. As he arrived to open the Ex-prisoners Interpretative Centre on the morning of Wednesday, June 11, 1997, Bobby Bates was shot dead.

Since he had been released from prison, Bobby went about doing good for others. He was a living witness to the fact that though anyone and everyone is capable of the greatest evil, anyone and everyone is also capable of the greatest good.

Ex-prisoners, particularly those with histories such as Bobby Bates, are often marked as the "untouchables" of society. Yet the whole foundation of our Christian belief — that God is love and all merciful and forgives us when we show remorse — seems to be ignored. Some Christians even go so far in their judgment of others that they pour out their scorn on those ex-prisoners who profess to be "saved" or "converted" during their long, solitary "dark night of the soul" in prison. We seem to forget that some of our greatest testimonies to the greatness of God down through the centuries have come from inside prison gates. I think there is something missing in our allegedly Christian society when mercy and compassion are not being shown to the marginalized people around us, such as prisoners, ex-prisoners, and the poor.

When Bobby Bates was murdered, most of the over four thousand ex-prisoners living in our midst felt very vulnerable. Along with many others, those of us in Peace People have been working with many ex-prisoners who are contributing so much to their communities. Now more than ever, we need to support ex-prisoners and their families so they can play their role as full citizens in our society. This is not to say that we ignore their victims. Rather, we acknowledge that prisoners are victims too. Prisoners suffer in their minds, and many return to society after a graced conversion as wise, deeply compassionate human beings. I have met such men and women who have become living examples of compassion and forgiveness to a society in need of healing and reconciliation.

Asking those who have lost loved ones during the Troubles to forgive those responsible is a hard yet necessary step. Forgiveness does not come easily. Forgiveness is a long process. We must allow people the chance to grow and to be "graced" into forgiveness in their own time and in God's good time.

Could not the politics of mercy and forgiveness be extended to all political prisoners? It is wrong that prisoners should be used as "pawns" in the politics of Northern Ireland. Their lives should not be on the table as part of the peace process negotiations, but should be dealt with in a more merciful and humane way. One possible approach to the political prisoners question is the recognition that they are "Emergency" prisoners, convicted under emergency laws. Since the Emergency is now drawing to a close, each case could be reviewed and a phased release of prisoners could begin immediately.

Some people in our community will argue that it is not the time for the release of the prisoners. The feelings of their victims must be taken into account, it is said. I believe we must take into account the feelings of the victims, but I must say that in all my years as a peace activist, I have been inspired by the spirit of forgiveness shown by so many who have suffered the loss of loved ones through our political violence. Most often, the loudest voices against prisoner releases are those who have not suffered. For my own part, I believe that the phased release of prisoners is long overdue.

As an ex-prisoner, Bobby Bates proved several truths to us all. First, people can show remorse and change their lives. Second, God is merciful and we are called as a community to show mercy and forgiveness to ourselves, each other, and the prisoners. Third, ex-prisoners have much to offer in developing a lasting peace process in Northern Ireland.

If Bobby Bates's death is not to be another statistic but rather a story of hope and a testimony to the greatness of God, we each need to name and reject our prejudices and our fears.

Only then will we come together to the dawn of peace and reconciliation as the people of God.

When this begins to happen, the death of all our loved ones will not be in vain.

8

The Parades

The mainly Catholic Garvaghy Road area and the Anglican church at Drumcree, both in Portadown, have come to epitomize the deep sectarian wounds in Northern Ireland in recent years. Each July, the Protestant Orange Order holds an annual church service at Drumcree and then insists on returning home by marching through Portadown's Catholic section of town, on the Garvaghy Road. The Garvaghy Road residents insist that the Orangemen are trespassing and violating their human rights by marching where they are not welcome. The intransigence results in a yearly "stand off" with ominous side effects for the whole region. During the 1996 Portadown parade, hundreds of rubber bullets were fired by the security forces at the Garvaghy Road residents and their supporters who were protesting the march. In 1997, a young Catholic man was kicked to death by loyalists, while nearby soldiers and police watched. In 1998, after ten Catholic churches were burned and three of them destroyed, British security forces enforced a ban on the Orange Order march. As tension mounted throughout the North, three Catholic brothers, Richard (ten), Mark (nine), and Jason (seven), were burned to death on July 12 in an arson attack in the town of Ballymoney. This reflection was written in June 1997.

Life is full of choices to be made and hard decisions to be taken. When uncertain about which way to choose, those of us from a Christian background can turn to the Scriptures and ask, "What would Jesus do?" I have been asking myself this question regarding the annual Orange Order parades in Portadown.

I keep remembering the following scriptural text: "If you are offering your gift at the altar and there remember that your brother has something against you, leave your gift there in front of the altar. First, go and be reconciled to your brother, then come and offer your gift" (Matt. 5:23).

This is indeed a hard saying. It is not just that I should make up with someone with whom I have a difference. It means much more than that. It commands me to go out and seek the

Previously unpublished.

person who has a difficulty with me. Now that is quite another matter! It's not easy being a Christian!

So, I'm an Orangeman all ready for July 12, attending the Church of Ireland service in Portadown. Can I really approach the altar with my gift, in good conscience, knowing that I have refused to talk face-to-face with my Catholic neighbors in the Garvaghy Residents Coalition Group?

Or maybe I'm a member of the Garvaghy Residents Coalition Group. When I go to Mass that Sunday in July can I really, in good conscience, approach the altar with my gift, knowing I have not proposed someone with whom the Orange Order could sit down with face-to-face? It's not easy being a Christian!

Is this scriptural command asking too much of both groups in this conflict? Is there too much pain for peace to be possible at this moment? As an outsider to Portadown, I can only try to empathize with the pain, anger, injustice, uncertainty, and fear, among both the Garvaghy Residents Coalition Group and the Orange Order members. It is understandable that both marchers and protestors feel they must stand up for their rights. Both groups feel aggrieved and determined not to give in. Both want to exercise their rights.

Again, I have to ask what have the Scriptures to say to these two Christian groups, who, although from different denominations, are brothers and sisters in Christ? What would Jesus say?

Both share a common Christian heritage. They also share together with the vast majority of people in Northern Ireland a deep fear and apprehension about what will happen in their own community and throughout Northern Ireland if a peaceful solution to the marches is not found and events escalate into all-out civil conflict.

The Scriptures are perfectly clear about what we are to do, both personally and collectively, as the people of God. We are to "love our enemy and do good to those who hate us." Above all, we are repeatedly told, "Do not be afraid." Do all that you can in the hope that by God's grace all will be well.

The Scriptures tell us to go out and make friends with our enemies and have the courage to compromise for the good of all people. It's not easy being a Christian! But that is the path to peace.

9

The Voice of Irish Women

It is fitting to commemorate and celebrate the lives of all the women of Ireland, North and South. In its long history, Ireland has had many inspiring daughters.

I take inspiration and courage from the words of one such foresister, Eva Gore-Booth, who reminds us that we are all the time evolving into something better. "We have to accustom our minds to the idea that we are not a being, but a becoming," she wrote. We are meant "to live something one has not yet become, for to live a thing is the only way of becoming it. It is not the self that one is that one must express in desire, thought, word, and deed, but the self that one desires to be."

Eva's words challenge me to dream the impossible, and then to live fully each moment aware that the dream is being fulfilled in me and in others too.

Many women (and men) since the 1798 rebellion have dreamed of a society, a country, and a world of justice and peace. I believe this desire is as fresh in the hearts of people today as it was in past generations.

The question then is, "How do we give birth to such a society, such a world?" In the past, the choice was between fight or flight. Some women and many men chose to fight. However, we now know that violence does not work. Furthermore, for those of us who have lived the last thirty years of the Troubles in Northern Ireland, we know that the insanity of violence can be stopped and reversed only by truth and love. As we enter the third millennium, we are discovering a third way, the way of active nonviolence. A commitment to nonviolence means we recognize the sanctity of human life and the Spirit of God living in every human being. We pledge ourselves never to violate or kill one another, wage war, oppress or threaten others. Nonviolence is not passive. No. It challenges us to work for equality

---

An address during the conference, "The Women of 1798–1998: A Commemoration and Celebration — from Rebellion to Reconciliation," at the Glencree Centre for Reconciliation, Dublin, February 27, 1998

and justice through unconditional love, steadfast truth-telling, and persistent reconciliation.

I believe Ireland is challenged to replace our growing culture of violence with a culture of nonviolence. This will not be entirely new to us. Indeed, Ireland has a long, if often overlooked, history of nonviolence. I often reflect how tragic it is that the world via the media hears so much of Ireland's tradition of violence, and is so unaware of our more important tradition of nonviolence. We have a history of ordinary women and men who have refused to use violence, who sought alternative ways to bring about social and political change. Ireland's nonviolence tradition gave the English language the term "boycott," and Michael Davitt's Land League campaign was an inspiration to the young Gandhi.

Building a new culture of nonviolence here in Ireland will be a hard but rewarding task. All our energies will be needed. We will have to join in solidarity with one another and with all people to create this new culture through our art, religion, and politics. But first and foremost, we will have to start with ourselves. Nonviolence begins in our hearts. As we strive for disarmed hearts, we can create a disarmed country and help disarm the world with new cultures of nonviolence.

Women in the North and the South will play a key role in the development of this new culture. Indeed the building of peace has been going on for a long time now. I am conscious of the role of peacemaking women in Northern Ireland. I hold in the deepest admiration so many women in the North, especially those women who live in the "troubled" areas of our cities. Their heroic and selfless efforts, caring for their families, serving their own local communities in the midst of terrible suffering, should not be left unrecorded in the annals of peace history. Their courage and strength is an example that the human spirit can rise again and again from great adversity and tragedy.

Herewith lies our hope for the future. Although many of these women choose not to be involved in party politics, they become community activists, beginning right in the home. Throughout the Troubles, we have often heard the voices of women calling for compassion instead of conflict, collaboration instead of coercion, and cooperation instead of competition. I believe that throughout the past thirty years, the strong pacifist values passed on by many women to their children have played a major role in preventing Northern Ireland from going down an even more violent road. We must remember that we are dealing with a deep ethnic/political problem with fear on all sides. It is somewhat of a miracle that we did not become like Bosnia.

Although it is a fact that the most socially deprived areas of the major cities in the North bore the brunt of the worst violence, for the most part they have kept strong family and community ties and support systems. Although this is changing as more women go on for further education and move into the workplace, there remains a deep consciousness among women that children come first and that child rearing is not only a great joy, but a sacrifice. To give children a sense of emotional peace and security, they need to feel valued and nourished at home. The things that make for peace and happiness are strong human relationships and networks of love and support. We all need these things in order to love and be loved and develop as fully mature human beings.

It is important that those in political and spiritual leadership positions listen to the voice of women in order that their needs and those of their families can best be met. If the voice of women is ignored, there is a real danger that the most needy will become further marginalized and forgotten.

In a recent University of Ulster study, "Women, Community and Politics in Northern Ireland," research showed that women identified the main issues facing their local communities as unemployment and poverty. They further identified the main problems facing Northern Ireland as unemployment first, and then the Troubles.

When asked how we can engage more women in political change, women replied, first, there must be more concern from politicians regarding social issues such as education, employment, health, and housing, and, second, women and their contributions must be valued.

Most Irish women, particularly from the economically deprived areas in the North, would not describe themselves as feminists. But in the past thirty years, as they have become politicized during the Troubles, women want to have their voices heard and their dignity upheld. They want to be treated equally. Since feminism maintains that women and men are equal, that women have the same rights as men, and that they are just as important human beings as men, then most Northern Irish women are indeed feminists, even though the word is rarely used in our daily vocabulary.

When women ask for the common attitude of men toward women to be changed, they do not want to replace the violence of patriarchy with matriarchy. They call for the equality of women and men. Women seek a redefinition of the relationship between women and men toward complete equality and mutuality. In our society, one of the largest institutionalized churches is structured by hierarchy and patriarchy, and all political and social institutions are male dominated and controlled. Many women are calling for the transformation of hierarchy, patriarchy, and male domination so that the human family can live as it was created to live — in equality, justice, and peace, for all women and men.

Women in Northern Ireland want to have their own needs and their families' needs met, and they wish to play their role in the social and political arenas. It is interesting to note that for many women, indeed I would argue for many nationalists in Northern Ireland, the question of Irish unity is well down their "wish list." So too, for many people, the cost of violence is too high a price to pay for a united Ireland. There is growing recognition that a united Ireland will not happen without the unity of our minds and hearts.

Northern Ireland is a perfect example of how people can never be united by coercion or violence. Unity among people begins with individuals who disarm their own hearts first. For many people, then, the question of Irish unity is a secondary consideration when faced with the more urgent and immediate problems of poverty, unemployment, division, and the urgent need for new political institutions which are fair and acceptable to most people living there.

This is not to dismiss, ignore, or invalidate the deep passion felt by many republicans and nationalists for a united Ireland, but rather an attempt to be honest and face the truth. Seventy years into partition, we are evolving into something new and different. Identities are changing. While some people describe themselves as "Irish" and others as "British," the shared Troubles have produced a growing and shared "Northern Irish" identity.

Today, in the North, many people would accept institutions based on equality, a Bill of Rights, together with North/South and East/West institutions. However, while these issues are under debate, the one issue upon which all women can totally agree is that political violence has had its day. The armed struggle must not be allowed to return. Peace is a right to which we are all entitled.

We women know that it is time to look to another way and to other goals. If we desire to be people of peace, joy, truth, and love and to build such communities, such a world, we need to begin to live every minute fully alive and in love and finally to learn that there is no other way to peace. Peace is the way.

10

Live Every Minute This Gift of Life: A Letter to My Son Luke

Dear Luke,

Today you picked a little yellow rosebud from the garden and carried it into the house to give it to me. Your little baby face beamed up at me as you gave me the rosebud. What joy that moment held for me! What joy knowing how deeply I love you! As I went to put that rosebud in water, I realized it had no stem, and that without water, it would never grow from a rosebud into a beautiful full rose, but that soon, all too soon, it would die.

I felt sad for a moment at this thought and as I watched you toddle across the room, I wondered how I might help you, my little rosebud, grow and blossom into manhood. What can I teach you? What can I say to you that will help you to grow up in this thorny world, and yet know peace, joy, and happiness, which, dear Luke, are the greatest treasures anyone can possess?

Always know, Luke, that you are deeply loved. You are loved by Daddy and me, and your brothers and sisters. But as you grow up and begin to ask questions for yourself, you will know that men and women have a need in their hearts for something more, something deeper than that found even in the very best of human love.

As you walk along a beach at night and listen to the waves lapping gently on the shore, or look up into a night sky at millions of stars, know too that the One who created all this created it for you because He loves you. You are part of this beautiful creation and you are beautiful, special, and unique in this universe. Love and believe in yourself, because only then can you love and believe in others.

Luke, do not be afraid to love others unselfishly. Yes, many times you will get your fingers pricked on the thorns of disappointment or rejection, but many more times you will pluck the rose of love and receive great happiness and joy from its

Published in *Peace by Peace,* Belfast, and in *Parade* magazine, September 1985.

sweet scent and color. Don't be afraid to risk loving and remember that, as the little rosebud needed the water to live, so
much more you and I and all the people of the world need to
love and be loved. Know that love is the greatest gift you personally can give to another fellow traveler along the thorny path
of life.

As you grow up in the Christian tradition, struggle each
day to be more Christ-like. Pray to be more loving, compassionate, courageous, gentle, and peaceful. Try to see Christ in
everyone, especially the suffering Christ, and serve and help to
remove the causes of that suffering where you can. Remember
it is a dead faith that has only words. Acts of love and compassion for the spiritually and materially poorest of the poor is
where true faith blossoms.

With ever so gentle steps, walk side-by-side with all travelers on this thorny path of life. They will differ from you in
color, creed (there are many paths to God), culture, and politics — but above all remember your fellow travelers have the
same needs as you. Our common humanity is far more important than any religious or political ideology. Treat every man
and woman justly and gently as you would have them treat you.

In your life, Luke, pray to be a just man. Your life is precious and sacred, Luke, and your first right as a human being
is your right to your life. So as you would ask natural justice
of your fellow travelers in respecting your right to life, then
you too must give justice and respect every person's right to
life. This means, my little son, that you must never kill another
human being.

It will not be easy for you to refuse to kill. Sadly, we live
in a world where those who refuse to kill and choose to live
nonviolent lives are looked upon as naive or as cowards. Yes, it
will take all your courage to walk unarmed, to refuse to hate
and kill, in this world which insists that you must have enemies
and be prepared to kill them before they kill you.

Stand tall and strong, armed only with love, dear Luke. Refuse to hate, refuse to have enemies, refuse to let fear master
your life. Only love can bring down the barriers of hate and enmity between people and nations. Hate and weapons only fuel
the fear and bring closer the day of war.

Let no one plant in your heart the false seed of pride in
any country's flag, a seed that produces the flower of nar-

row nationalism which grows so wildly, trampling and killing all life around it. Remembers always, Luke, people are more important than countries.

I would not give one hair of your precious head for any country. You are more important than any country. And if I feel this passionate love for you, and for my other children, Mark, Joanne, Marie-Louise, and John, I too feel passionately for the lives of all children, children who die today of starvation in Ethiopia, children in Moscow and children in New York who are told they must be enemies and may end up someday killing each other in the name of the flag.

Remember, Luke, you have no country. The world is your country. You have not only two brothers and two sisters but millions of brothers and sisters.

Pray also for the gift of wisdom. It is a wise person who soon comes to know that the human family's real enemies are injustice, war, starvation, and poverty. But wise people also know that it is only by people becoming different and thinking in new ways that these things will change.

When human life is held as so sacred that no one can kill, then justice will reign in people's hearts and in all lands. Wars will be no more. Justice will mean that no one has too much, while some have nothing. Greed and selfishness will turn into feeding the hungry and removing all poverty. It is possible, Luke, to change to this kind of world. You just have to refuse to accept the old ways of thinking and doing things and begin to think and act in a way more in tune with the magnificent goodness in humanity. All people know today that killing and starvation are wrong. It is just that not enough are prepared to change themselves and to work on making things different.

And now, my little son, before you fall asleep, let me say the most important thing of all to you. Be happy, be joyous, live every minute of this beautiful gift of life. When suffering comes into your life, and sadly I cannot, much as I would love to, protect you from all suffering, and when you come through the winter of your life, remember that summer will return, the sun will shine again, and the road will be covered with beautiful, very beautiful, yellow roses of love.

God bless you and keep you, my little Luke.

Mummy

II

Peace in the World

In Amsterdam in 1994, at a celebration marking the 125th anniversary of the birth of Mahatma Gandhi.

11

Grassroots Peacemaking
in a World of Ethnic Conflict

The ethnic conflicts tearing our world apart are perhaps the greatest challenge before us all. How can we solve nonviolently some of the deep ethnic conflicts in our world today and thus give hope and inspiration to each other?

When the Soviet Union collapsed, there was a sense around the world that one repression had stopped and a new opportunity had arisen for the human family to begin to make peace, to divert those vast resources allocated to militarism and redirect them to those areas in the world suffering most from poverty, violence, and environmental destruction. At that moment, there was hope in the world that we were a family and perhaps we could make it together.

Tragically, within a very short time, we began to hear of countries in the Soviet bloc such as Chechnya, countries which had been held together by military might, suddenly making their voices heard. Yugoslavia's dissolution followed soon after. Suddenly new republics, like Slovenia and Bosnia-Herzegovina, appeared, having survived seventy years of repression. But as we learned, they survived decades of repression with their historic hatreds intact. The people were armed and internal conflicts quickly flared up again.

At this point, the superpowers realized that nuclear and conventional weapons and armies were absolutely useless in these situations. One cannot drop a nuclear bomb on an ethnic conflict (nor anywhere else, for that matter). The weapons we have developed to solve our problems are no longer of any use to us.

This became evident to me in 1995 when I traveled to Burundi in Africa. I was part of a small delegation of Irish women who were invited to see the situation firsthand. At the time, there was growing international pressure to send in UN military forces in order to prevent Burundi from following

Remarks for the Annual Tanner Lecture, at the University of California at Riverside, March 4, 1996.

Rwanda down the road to genocide. The pressure was exac-
erbated by the international press, which broadcast television
images of refugees fleeing from Burundi.

When we arrived, we witnessed terrible problems in Burundi. People were fleeing the violence. The army had killed
many people. We asked the people, "How can the outside
world help? What can we do?" They responded simply, "Don't
send us any guns. Don't send us any military forces. The place
is awash with guns. But in the refugee camps, our children
need food, and we do not have enough money to buy ourselves
food. Yet a child with a few cents can buy a weapon. The West
has given us weapons for too long. Do not send them to us
anymore." This was a plea from the heart. The Burundi people
said their ethnic/political problems cannot be solved by further
violence.

It is important to recognize that we are all interconnected
with these ethnic conflicts. What happens in a place like Burundi affects all of us around the world. We play a key role
in Burundi because 85 percent of the weapons sold to Third
World nations come from the United States and the European
community.

Eighty-five percent of these weapons in the Third World
come from the wealthy First World nations. We must delude
ourselves no longer. We are arming the Third World. In return, a high percentage of their budgets and international aid
are coming back to the West. While some of these countries
cannot feed their people, they can and do buy our guns and
send our money back to us. This is so unjust. It causes so much
suffering. The world's people need to unite their voice to stop
this genocide of the poor.

In the early 1990s, I traveled with a delegation of Nobel
Peace Prize laureates to the Thai/Burma border. In the refugee
camps, we heard the stories of women who had been taken
out of their villages and forced to serve the Burmese soldiers. Many of these women told us how they had been raped
by the Burmese soldiers. They had witnessed many killings
and the torture of dissidents by the Burmese soldiers. Here
again Western interests are interwoven in this ethnic/political
conflict.

In the mid-1970s, Western oil companies invested in Burma,
saving the Burmese military from the brink of financial col-

lapse. The military then used the oil revenue to buy weapons to control and kill many Burmese. We are fast moving into a world where big businesses control national and international economies. They quickly become more politically powerful than national and international governments and political institutions and find themselves at the service of brutal military forces.

Burma's Nobel Peace Prize winner Aung San Suu Kyi has stood up to the military authorities for years, enduring death threats, harassment, and house arrest, yet she continues to speak for peace and democracy. People all around the world know of Suu Kyi and her tremendous sacrifice for human rights. She is a symbol of hope for the people of Burma that someday their suffering will end, that peace will be restored to their land. But peace comes with a high price, and people such as Aung San Suu Kyi risk their lives when they stand up against vast military power to speak for truth and justice.

There are few people in the world who carry a moral authority as profound as this "Lady of Burma." Imprisoned by the military under house arrest for almost six years and refused visits from her husband, Michael, and her two sons, Alexander and Kim, for many years, nonetheless Aung San Suu Kyi continues to speak for peace. One cannot imagine her loneliness, suffering, and pain. We can only give thanks for such a wonderful human being, for the hope she gives in the face of such deep conflict, for her courage in the face of fear and oppression, and for her compassion and self-sacrifice in the face of cruelty and power.

Burma's military authorities cannot crush the people forever. In time, they will admit the truth that ethnic/political conflicts such as theirs cannot be solved through violence, militarism, and paramilitarism. All wars and violence come to an end, and the sooner the Burmese military sits down at the table of reconciliation and begins to dialogue with Aung San Suu Kyi and all the parties in the conflict, the sooner the terrible suffering of the Burmese people will end.

⁕⊗⊙

Of course, we too have deep ethnic/political problems in Northern Ireland. But too often the media and others imply that our conflict lies solely between the British government and the Irish Republican Army. This is not true! When the Troubles began in 1969, people died on the streets of Belfast before the British army was brought in. In 1969, when the British army was brought in, the IRA was barely in existence and unarmed. Nearly two years passed before the IRA became a real guerrilla armed force. We should lay to rest all the imagined intrigues about the British government, the British army, and the IRA.

Northern Ireland is a community of only one and a half million people. One million are Protestants and unionists who want to maintain links with the British government, who would die before they would agree to a united Ireland. The minority community of Catholics and nationalists represent one-third of the population and are aggrieved by the fact that seventy-five years ago Ireland was partitioned and they were separated from their hinterland. They are very conscious that they have been treated for a long time as second-class citizens.

A deep fear has grown between these two distinct ethnic groups who have lived apart for the past seventy-five years. As the population figures shift toward an equal balance, as the unionists begin to lose control, these ethnic divisions can quickly turn deadly. Because we have been divided for so long, because the level of fear is so high, and because the siege mentality controls us, many people in Northern Ireland have been quite capable of killing one another. We must never underestimate the human capacity for murder. Each one of us would be murderous under certain circumstances, and that is why we all need to learn and embrace nonviolence.

It is fine to celebrate our diversity and our roots, but we must also rise above those ideas that divide us to understand our most basic identity, our common membership in the human family. What we have in common is more important than what divides us. As we focus on our common unity, we can build bridges and work together. Then we will remember that we are more important than the flags, languages, customs, and religions that divide us.

In order to overcome the fear of difference and to celebrate diversity, we need to study and practice nonviolence. Over the years, as I have struggled to find the meaning of life in Northern Ireland during this particular historical period, I have been forced to question everything. I grew up in an area where some people accepted as fact that young men should join the IRA and that war can be morally justified. I grew up seeing state injustice firsthand. I grew up knowing that I could not sit back, that no one should sit back and do nothing because doing nothing in the face of state injustice is wrong itself. But could I ever take up arms?

To deal with these issues, I went on my own spiritual journey and came to recognize that each human life is sacred. We are all involved in the mystery of life. We are given life as a gift, and we have no right to take that gift from another human being. As a Christian, I discovered the greatest symbol of nonviolence is Jesus hanging on a cross, saying, "Love your enemy; do not kill."

I had been deeply confused about what to do to help people and sought the advice of a local priest. "Father," I asked, "is it right to take up a gun to stand for justice and oppose this state violence?" I was deeply concerned and knew I had to do something.

"Pray about it, Mairead," the priest said to me.

So I went to a church and sat down before the crucifix. At this stage, I was on the brink of resorting to violence. I looked up at the crucifix. Quite clearly from the crucifix came the message of Jesus: "Love one another. Love your enemy. Thou shalt not kill. Do good to those that hate you." I knew then and there what Christianity is all about. We love our enemies; we do not kill them. We go out to transform our enemies into friends. The power of love, not violence, is the instrument for change. It was a few years later before I began to use the word "nonviolence," but I knew that day that violence is not the way of Jesus.

I came to nonviolence then by going into a quiet place and asking, "What would Jesus do? " That's all any Christian can ask. And it's the question every Christian should ask regarding not only personal life problems, but the deep-seated ethnic/political conflicts that divide and destroy us. The answer is always astonishingly simple and real: "Thou shalt not kill. Love your enemies."

⌒◈⌒

I believe that the major religions of the world have their roots in love, tolerance, respect, and nonviolence. Therefore I passionately believe that the only way to accomplish real change is through the power of love operating in the world.

How do we solve our ethnic problems without killing each other? At home in Northern Ireland, we try to accomplish this grassroots work by teaching nonviolence at every level in our society, with courses on conflict resolution, prejudice reduction, and human rights. This is a new direction for us. By teaching respect for life and human diversity, we are paving the way for a more tolerant and compassionate future.

I firmly believe that we must teach nonviolence everywhere in the world, in every home, community, university, and nation. We must begin now building a nonviolent world.

In Northern Ireland, we desperately need to build community. The only solution to a deep ethnic conflict, the only way to reduce fear, is to increase tangible human contact by bringing divided people together. We have the Internet and television, but they cannot replace human contact. That would be a lazy and dangerous road to take. Human beings need to love and be loved, to feel a sense of dignity, acceptance, and respect, and this can be received only through human contact.

Respect for human dignity will be realized when people communicate directly with one another. For this to occur, there will not be dramatic overnight solutions. Belfast, for example, has fourteen walls that, sadly, keep our people segregated. Our schools are segregated too. This division leads to further fear and mistrust. We have to do all we can to build trust. One of our Peace People programs offers transportation by bus for loyalist and republican wives and children so they can visit their relatives in prisons. This bus takes people from one community to another community and allows individuals who often fear each other to sit, ride, and communicate with one another.

In Northern Ireland, we seem to have lost the ability to hear the other person. When the first cease-fire was called, I went to the Falls Road, where the Catholic community was saying, "The cease-fire is wonderful! We can move forward for a real change." There was a sense of euphoria. Then I went to the Protestant Shankill Road where a young minister confided to me, "It's a sad day for the Protestant people here. A deal has been made between the British and the IRA." He was fearful, like the people, that somehow his community was being sold out.

Our inability to listen has made us deaf and blind to what

others are feeling and saying. Our very language divides us. Our Protestant and Catholic traditions use language very differently. The word "justice," for example, has a completely different meaning for Protestants and Catholics in Northern Ireland. When we attempt to tackle issues such as prisoner release or police reform, we approach them from different perspectives and priorities. This makes the work much more difficult. We have got to learn to listen and stay together as we move forward.

Part of our work now for the creation of a peaceful future is building community. Once people feel that they can and do make a difference and are important in their communities, they feel empowered. How do we give people in their local communities that sense of power? We must build communities nonviolently from the bottom up in order to break down at the top the ethnic politics that divide us.

Only when the six hundred villages of Northern Ireland begin to mobilize, solve local problems, elect local citizens to represent them, and develop their own resources and finances for employment will a nonviolent society be born. Financial resources and power at the grassroots level allow communities to feel that they themselves can make a difference. Then they can solve their own problems nonviolently.

If we return to a devolved government based on ethnic division, we may have a stalemate for the next ten or fifteen years, but someone will come along to remind us of our differences and then, once again, our fragile country will blow apart. Changing politics from the bottom up is therefore not only idealistic, but essential and practical for a peaceful future in Northern Ireland.

Once the guns are taken out of Irish politics, once everyone is brought into the dialogue, we will go forward. As a Northern Irish identity evolves, as the two communities come together for resolution and change, our identities will change. We will become who we already are.

Still the unionists fear they will be pulled into a united Ireland, but there will be no united Ireland in the foreseeable future. The nationalists fear they will be pulled back into an unjust government as before, but there is no going back to injustice. The hope lies in the growing recognition that there must be a pluralist political movement for the two main traditions. Majority rule in divided societies is not democracy and doesn't work.

We are moving forward in Northern Ireland. We have a great deal of hope. We hope to solve our ethnic political problem nonviolently and thus offer a safe future for our people. There will be hiccups of course. Changing our attitudes about one another requires a lifelong commitment and all sides must be prepared to give a little. It will not be easy, but we have no alternative.

But even in the midst of devastation, there is hope in our world. On the streets of Burundi, I saw great hope. Young North Americans were in the refugee camps with their mobile phones and aid trucks, working in partnership with the Burundi people, helping them. In the forests of Burma, I saw young North Americans helping prodemocracy students work the Internet and learn from them. We are embarking on a two-way process now, and we all have to learn from each other.

I am hopeful that His Holiness the Dalai Lama has offered to dialogue with the Chinese authorities regarding the situation in Tibet, and that in spite of the repression in Tibet, the Dalai Lama and the Buddhists in Tibet and in other countries have stood firmly by their nonviolent tradition of compassion and respect for life. I hope the Chinese authorities will take up that offer and sit together around a table and begin to build trust. I am very sure that the Tibetan and Chinese brothers and sisters can begin to solve these deep problems. That would give great hope to the world. China is a wonderful country and is going to play a very important role in the future, and I'm sure that given the opportunity, the Chinese people themselves would want their government to solve their problems through dialogue and negotiation. If we could have a real peace process between Tibet and China, and in Northern Ireland, and in the Middle East, just as we have had in South Africa, that would give great hope to the world. We are all interconnected, and we all need hope.

As Martin Luther King Jr. tried to build the "beloved community," we need to encourage leaders to build the beloved community with all the nations of the world. And we need to do so where we are, at the grassroots level, so that our ethnic divisions will be healed.

We all know what to do: make real changes and work tirelessly as we do in the streets of Belfast. We knock on doors. We sell our little paper and we build peace in Belfast one home, one family, at a time. In the United States, in Burundi, in Burma, in Tibet, everywhere, ordinary peacemakers are doing that same grassroots peacework. Together, we will create a new world.

12

Gandhi and the Ancient Wisdom of Nonviolence

January 30, 1998

My dear sisters and brothers,

It was a great privilege and joy for me to be with you all in India and to have been given the honor of addressing the Gandhian movement on August 15, 1997, the fiftieth anniversary of India's independence.

I thank you all for your kindness and shall always remember India and my very good friends there. One particular memory will always remain with me: at the midnight hour on the fiftieth anniversary of independence, when I read the pledge of nonviolence with over three thousand men, women, and children.

I was deeply conscious, as an advocate of nonviolence, that for me, this ceremony was a continuation of the most important connection between Ireland's tradition of nonviolence and India's tradition of nonviolence. I felt deep joy in being part of this heroic endeavor by Gandhi's sons and daughters to further his work and vision in the building of a nonviolent culture for India and humanity.

I saw for myself, during my visit to India, that the spirit of Gandhi is fully alive. Over half a century after his death, Gandhi continues to inspire many millions of people. On January 30, 1998, the fiftieth anniversary of his assassination, many people in India and around the world will remember, celebrate, and give thanks for the life of India's great son, the prophet of nonviolence, Mohandas Gandhi, the Mahatma. Together with Martin Luther King, Jr., and Mother Teresa, Mahatma Gandhi ranks as one of the greatest figures of this century.

I believe that Gandhi's greatest legacy to both India and humanity was the example of a life filled with the Spirit of

---

An open letter to friends and grassroots leaders in India, marking the fiftieth anniversary of Mahatma Gandhi's assassination, published in Indian peace journals and in *Fellowship* magazine, June 1998.

God, a life lived in the Spirit of nonviolence, a life lived every minute fully alive, in deep awareness of the presence of God, in, about, and all around us. It was this loving Spirit which enabled Gandhi to become one of history's greatest prophets and practitioners of nonviolence.

I think of the words of St. Paul to the Corinthians: "Didn't you realize that you were God's temple and that the Spirit of God was living among you?" Gandhi lived the truth of these words. He took time to purify his own bodily temple through discipline and self-denial. He set aside time to be still, to be silent, to accept God's peace, to allow God to fill him up with love. He acquired a deep love and respect not only for human life but for all sentient beings. He recognized that each person is a sacred temple of the Spirit of love, that we are all equal, that all of us are sisters and brothers of one another. I too have come to believe, as Gandhi did, in the wisdom of nonviolence, that to tell a lie, to violate, hurt, or kill another human person, is to violate, hurt, and kill the Spirit of God alive in every human being.

Gandhi realized that the spirit of nonviolence begins within us and moves out from there. The life of active nonviolence is the fruit of an inner peace and spiritual unity already realized within us, and not the other way around. I have come to believe with Gandhi that through our own personal inner conversion, our own inner peace, we are sensitized to care for God, ourselves, each other, for the poor, and for our world, and then we can become true servants of peace in the world. Herein lies the power of nonviolence. As our hearts are disarmed by God of our inner violence, they become God's instruments for the disarmament of the world. Without this inner conversion, we run the risk of becoming embittered, disillusioned, despairing, apathetic, or simply burnt out, especially when our work for peace and justice appears to produce little or no results or seems trifling in comparison with the injustice we see all around us. With this conversion, we learn to let go of "all desires," including the destructive desire to see results.

For many people, this ancient wisdom of the heart, the wisdom of nonviolence, may seem too religious and too idealistic in today's hard-headed world of politics and science. But I believe with Gandhi that we need to take an imaginative leap forward, toward a fresh and generous idealism, for the sake of all humanity, that we need to renew this ancient wisdom of nonviolence, to strive for a disarmed world, and to create new cultures of nonviolence.

As we enter the third millennium, we need to apply this ancient wisdom to politics, economics, and science. For many, particularly in the West, increased materialism and unprecedented consumerism have not led to inner peace or happiness. And although technology has given us many benefits, it has not helped us distinguish between what enhances life and humanity and what destroys life and humanity. The time has come to return to the ancient wisdom of nonviolence.

When we examine where we are today, given the politics and technology of violence, we can only conclude that we live in an insane world.

Is it not insanity to go on producing nuclear and conventional weapons that, if used, can destroy millions of people, if not the whole planet?

Is it not insanity to spend billions of dollars to maintain these arsenals while millions of children die of disease and starvation each year? When, according to the United Nations, sixty thousand children die every day of starvation, even though the world's governments have the resources and capability of ending starvation and misery immediately?

Is it not insanity to implement sanctions on some countries when their only effect is to punish the most vulnerable and weak, the infants, the children, the sick, the elderly, and the destitute? Is it not insanity, for example, that because of UN sanctions against Iraq, forty-five hundred Iraqi children die every month, according to the UN?

Is it not insanity to produce and export weapons of destruction to poor Third World countries, instead of exporting food, medicine, and the necessities of life? Is it not insanity that the United States and the European Union, of which Britain is a major arms contributor, now export 70 percent of the world's arms to poor Third World countries? Some of these countries bankrupt themselves to pay for these arms, which in many cases will be used by military regimes against their own people.

Is it not insanity, for example, that India's government continues to waste so many resources on militarism, while so many of their people are in need of the basics necessities of life?

Is it not insanity to pollute the air, poison the oceans, dump radioactive materials, destroy the ozone, send plutonium into outer space, and destroy the environment?

Yes, it is insanity. I believe with Gandhi that the insanity of violence can be stopped only by the sanity of nonviolence. The time has come to renew our commitment personally, politically, economically, and internationally to the ancient wisdom of nonviolence.

⌒∞⌒

As we move into the third millennium, we are beginning to realize that the human family is multiethnic, multicultural, and pluralistic in nature, and that if we are going to survive and develop, we will need to learn to live together nonviolently.

In Rwanda, Bosnia, and to a lesser degree in my own Northern Ireland, we have lived the consequences of deep ethnic, political violence. We see how injustice and militarism breed fear and hatred and release murderous passions, drowning out all reason, compassion, and mercy. Most people prefer to believe that they are themselves too "civilized" to carry out such horrors, but we need to honestly face up to Gandhi's truth that each one of us, while capable of the greatest good, is also, given the right circumstances, capable of the greatest evil.

In facing such problems, we know that the "old" ways of violence, war, and militarism no longer work. Violence does not solve anything. It only leads to further violence. Since Gandhi's lifetime, it is clear that violence, war, and militarism only lead to further violence, war, and militarism down the line. Building, maintaining, and selling weapons of mass destruction only deepen our insanity of violence. We can not keep spending billions of the peoples' money, maintaining these huge arsenals of destruction and ignoring the world's poor, without going deeper down the spiral of violence.

Today, fifty years after Gandhi's death, we are faced with a choice. We can continue down the spiral of violence by supporting systemic injustice, turning away from the starving masses, maintaining our weapons, and using militaristic reactions to current political conflicts, which we know will only lead to an increase in hatred and violence, *or* we can choose the way of nonviolence by renouncing our violence, dismantling our weapons, reversing our imperial domination over others, feeding the world's hungry, and sowing seeds of peace and justice. Gandhi said, "There is no hope for the aching world except through the narrow and straight path of nonviolence."

If we want to reap the harvest of peace and justice in the future, we will have to sow seeds of nonviolence, here and now, in the present.

All of us need to take responsibility for the world's violence and, like Gandhi, pledge our lives to the nonviolent transformation of the world, to resolve these insane crises through the wisdom of nonviolence.

Gandhi taught that nonviolence does not mean passivity. It is not just a political tactic. It is the most daring and courageous way of living, and it is the only hope for the world. Nonviolence is an active way of life which always rejects violence and killing and instead applies the force of love and truth as a means to transform conflict and the root causes of conflict. Nonviolence demands creativity. It pursues dialogue, seeks reconciliation, listens to the truth in our opponents, rejects militarism, and remains open to God's Spirit transforming us socially and politically.

⤛∞⤜

Getting to the root cause of the conflict is now the greatest challenge facing my own people in Northern Ireland. We need now to build a culture of genuine nonviolence and real democracy. This can only happen through consensus politics built by the people and courageous political leadership by the government on human rights issues.

Thirty years ago, if the Northern Ireland government had implemented civil rights instead of responding to conflict by ever increasing repression, emergency legislation, and outright militarization, the savage violence we have known would never have erupted. Today, while we are thankful that the peace process has begun, we are deeply conscious that the same problems that were there in 1968 still remain, awaiting a solution in an atmosphere of mistrust deepened by thirty years of unnecessary violence.

The only thing that we have learned is that violence makes things worse. Yet people remain afraid to take the steps required to remove the elements of militarization which maintain our state of fear. The time has come for the government, rather than minor political parties, to take a lead and to act with fearlessness and imagination. For example, the removal of large sections of emergency legislation and the immediate release of large numbers of prisoners who were convicted under emergency legislation would help the process of building a nonviolent culture in Northern Ireland.

All people in Northern Ireland have their part to play in building a more democratic, nonviolent culture from the ground up. We know that power divided between ethnically based political parties and upheld by armed security forces is not a real, lasting solution. Until trust and consensus is built among the Northern Irish people themselves, there can be no real solution. To enable consensus politics to develop, we need to empower people where they live. This means devolving financial resources and political power down to the community level. One of the greatest blocks to change is fear. This fear can be removed only when people feel their voices are being heard and when they have a say in their own lives and communities.

⌒⊗⌒

But Gandhi's challenge of nonviolence is not only a necessity for ourselves, for Northern Ireland; it is a challenge before the whole of humanity. Fifty years after his death, Gandhi challenges us to a new millennium of nonviolence, to build cultures of nonviolence. This is not an impossible dream. In order to create new cultures of nonviolence, each of us has to play an active role. There are several basic steps that we can take toward the pursuit of this dream.

First, we need to teach nonviolence to the children of the world — in India, in Northern Ireland, and everywhere. Recently, twenty Nobel Peace Prize laureates asked the United Nations to declare the first decade of the new millennium as "a culture of nonviolence for the children of the world," in the hope that every nation will spend money educating its children in the way of nonviolent conflict resolution. I was pleased during my visit to India to launch this movement and to see the Gandhian movement giving a strong example to the world by teaching nonviolence to the children in the schools.

Second, as individuals, we can exorcize violence and untruth from our own lives. We can stop supporting systemic violence and militarism and dedicate ourselves to nonviolent social change. We can take public stands for disarmament and justice and take new risks for peace.

Third, we can urge the media to stop sensationalizing violence and instead to highlight peaceful interactions, promote nonviolence, and uphold those who strive for real peace.

Fourth, we can embrace the wisdom of nonviolence that lies underneath each of the world's religions. Every religion contains the ancient truth of nonviolence. Every religion needs to begin more and more to teach and promote nonviolence and to worship the God of nonviolence. Gandhi said, "If religion does not teach us how to achieve the conquest of evil by overcoming it with goodness, it teaches us nothing." The world's religions need to come together in dialogue and respect, because there can be no world peace until the great religions make peace with one another. Perhaps the greatest contribution that those of us who come from a Christian tradition can make is to throw out the old just war theory, embrace the nonviolence of Jesus, refuse to kill one another, and truly follow his commandment to "love our enemies."

Fifth, we need to pursue Gandhi's dream of unarmed, international peacemaking teams which resolve international conflict not through military solutions but nonviolent means. The world's governments need not only to reject military solutions, but to support nonviolent solutions and create international nonviolent conflict resolution programs.

More than anything else, Gandhi inspires me by his great love for the poor. Perhaps the greatest contribution we can pay to Gandhi is to work to eliminate poverty from the face of the earth. Gandhi said that poverty is the worst form of violence. His memorial in India contains his parting advice, which we need to keep before us every day of our lives: "Recall the face of the poorest person you have ever seen, and ask yourself if the next step you take will be of any use to that person."

As we remember his death and celebrate his life, we dedicate ourselves to the wisdom of nonviolence. Shortly before his death, Gandhi said, "We are constantly being astonished these days at the amazing discoveries in the field of violence. But I maintain that far more undreamt of and seemingly impossible discoveries will be made in the field of nonviolence."

With Gandhi, we can share great hope in a future filled with peace. Like Gandhi, each one of us can make that hope a reality by pursuing new discoveries in the field of nonviolence, building cultures of nonviolence, creating a new millennium of nonviolence, and becoming, like Gandhi, teachers, practitioners, and prophets of nonviolence.

As we exit the second millennium, we find hope in the many excellent achievements and discoveries made by the millions of our sisters and brothers who have gone before us. They have, by their examples, enriched, inspired, and encouraged us to build lives of joy and peace for ourselves and all people.

May the God of Mahatma Gandhi, the God of nonviolence, bless India, Northern Ireland, and us all with peace, fill us with hope, and lead us and all humanity into a new world of nonviolence.

Siochain, Shanthi, Salaam, Peace,
Mairead

13

Remembering Auschwitz

In January 1988 I received a request from Elie Wiesel to join him, his wife, his friends, and some fellow Nobel laureates on a visit to Auschwitz. As a teenager, Elie Wiesel was taken from his home to Auschwitz, the best-known German concentration camp, where he witnessed the death of his family and unforgettable evil. I accepted his invitation, along with my friend Betty Williams Perkins, and joined a group of fifty-six people who flew to Cracow, Poland.

On arrival in Cracow, we were met by Lech Walesa and members of Solidarity. Walesa looked well and happy as he greeted us with a smile. Then we traveled by coach some thirty miles to Auschwitz and Birkenau.

My companion during the ride was a gentleman named Bernie. When we began to talk about the Jewish Holocaust, his eyes filled with tears and he shook slightly as the nightmarish memories overpowered him. I said I was so sorry for what was done to the Jewish people by Christians, and I asked him to forgive me and all Christians for what we had done. He smiled and gently pressed my hand. There was no anger, no bitterness, only complete forgiveness in his steady eyes.

On arrival at Auschwitz we passed through the exterior barbed-wire fences, once electrified and patrolled by dogs and armed soldiers. The long cobblestoned streets were lined on both sides with two-story red-brick numbered buildings. We laid wreaths at the wall where people had been lined up daily to be shot or hung for being Jewish, or too sick or too young or too old to work. One building contained hundreds of pictures of the unspeakable evil carried out by humans on fellow humans in this place of terror. As we walked through the camp, Bernie held my arm, and I thanked God that he had sent this friend to help me through this hellish place, heavy with memories of unbelievable horror, suffering, and death.

First printed in *Peace by Peace,* in Belfast, April 1988, and later reprinted in many international publications.

We walked into the gas chambers. To stand in this chamber and remember that men, women, and little children were burned in their millions; to know that the sky lit up each night with the flames and that the air was thick with the smell of their burning flesh — I could only cry in my heart, "O God, forgive us for what we do to one another."

In the gas chamber, a rabbi and a priest led our group in prayer. Suddenly in the distance a church bell rang. It struck me forcibly and shamed me deeply to know that forty-five years ago, Jewish people would listen to church bells calling Christians, mostly Catholics, to prayer. They would watch as some of those who tortured and murdered fellow humans went off to church. Without the knowledge and support of the local communities, these pits of hell could not have been kept running. They too would answer the church bell and pray. How few there were who raised their voices and tried to do something to stop the extermination of the Jewish people, but thank God for them. Hitler's mad policy to exterminate Europe's Jews was made all the more possible by the multitude's silence, cemented by the anti-Semitism of Polish and European Christians.

While we pray that the Jewish people will, and do, forgive, we all must join with them in making certain that the world never forgets what happened at Auschwitz so that it never happens again. Anyone who does not believe in evil should stand in Auschwitz. They will see the great evil we are all capable of and learn to acknowledge the dark side of our nature which can lead us to terrible, evil deeds. Auschwitz shows us the strange paradox of humanity: we are all capable of great goodness by the grace of God, but we are all capable too of great evil. When we let anger, hatred, racism, greed, fear, and nationalism blind us to our common humanity, we are indeed capable of unspeakable evil. It is all too easy to point the finger and condemn others. Surely the lesson to be learned is that we must look to our own lives and societies and be vigilant in working for human rights, justice, and peace.

Even in our own time we witness great evil. Recently, here in Northern Ireland, we have seen on television an array of violence: an angry mob that beat two British soldiers and handed them over to be stripped and brutally murdered by the IRA; the murder of three unarmed IRA members in Gibraltar by the security forces; the bombing and shooting by a loyalist gunman of Catholics as they buried their dead in the Milltown cemetery; the murder of a young Protestant girl by the IRA as she drove home with her boyfriend; and the sectarian murder by loyalist paramilitaries of a young Catholic farmer. This evil cycle of killing can be broken only by people refusing to hate and to kill and by working nonviolently for social justice.

Recently, the world has also witnessed the brutality of Israeli soldiers beating Palestinian stone throwers. We are deeply concerned by a recent report by Rev. Canon Riah Abud El-Assal, documenting the cases of torture of Palestinian children in Israeli military prisons. The people of Israel, many who themselves were victims of torture, are challenged now to uphold human rights for their Palestinian sisters and brothers by giving them justice and the right to self-determination.

Before leaving the camps, in the midst of such ugliness, I looked about for some sign of beauty. The cobblestoned roads were lined with beautiful, tall poplar trees. They seemed to reach up to the sky. I felt that they, like myself, were reaching up to cry out, "Where are you God?" I looked around at my companions and I knew that God doesn't live up in the sky. God lives in us and in each one of our sisters and brothers. People are the temples of God, and therein real beauty lives, if only we have eyes to see.

From Auschwitz, we traveled to Cracow to visit the Ramu synagogue. Standing in the courtyard, I glanced up at a nearby wall. There was a memorial plaque to both grandparents of my fellow traveler Bernie. When I pointed out the plaque, he stood fixed to the ground, his eyes shining in amazement. He had been unaware of its existence. I don't believe in coincidence, but I do believe in miracles. God had led Bernie from New York to Auschwitz to find some trace of both sets of his beloved grandparents. He rushed off to find a camera. His photograph will be treasured back in New York by his children and his children's children. No doubt the picture and the story of the Holocaust will be passed from generation to generation. It is right that the Jewish people and all of us should remember, but it is right too that they and we should decide to forgive. Through forgiveness and reconciliation, there is a way forward for humanity, for Jew and Gentile, American and Russian, and everyone. The list is endless.

I am certain that it is only when humanity stops being afraid, stops hating and starts loving, only then can our hearts and minds become open to the possibility of a new and more just world.

Through love we can come to know that human life is sacred and that we have no right to respond to violence with further retaliation. Then there will be no more Auschwitzes, no more Belfast riots, no more Middle East conflicts.

There is still so much for us to do. But when we get tired, we will remember Auschwitz and find new strength to carry on the work for peace.

14

From the Former Yugoslavia to Northern Ireland

One morning in the former Yugoslavia during the fall of 1991, while the Yugoslav army was bombing the cities of Croatia, just after bombing the Parliament building in Zagreb itself, I spoke with the bishop of Zagreb.

"As the Serb-dominated federal army go along, taking over the villages they have bombed," he said, "they kill old people who won't move from their homes. One old lady's brutalized body was found hanging upon a wooden cross with her arms outstretched. Over two hundred churches have been destroyed, whole villages have been cleared and ruined, and whole cities cut off and surrounded by federal army troops. Innocent civilians, including little children, are forced to take shelter underground as the bombs fall around them. The city of Vokavar has over forty thousand people suffering like that. They have no electricity, water, food, or medicines. This is an army second only to the Soviet Union's military might, which is causing the genocide of the Croat people in a frenzied attempt to hold on to 'old' style communist rule and thereby denying people their right to democracy."

"Tell the world," the bishop pleaded, "to do everything it can to stop the federal forces and demand their withdrawal from Croatia. The army has killed thousands of people. They have bombed hospitals. This is not like Northern Ireland." As he said these words, he began to cry.

Yes, even bishops cry. In times like these, some must surely ask themselves, "Has the world gone mad?"

I was in Zagreb to meet local peace activists and to attend the Federal Council of the Transnational Nonviolent Radical Party. I gave enthusiastic consent to the resolutions passed by the council urging the immediate recognition of the republics of the former Yugoslavia that have democratically proclaimed their independence and the application of economic sanctions

Published in *Peace by Peace*, Belfast, November 1991.

if the Serbian-dominated federal army does not immediately cease the bombing of Croatia.

On the return flight to Northern Ireland, the bishop's words came back to me. I read with a heavy heart the news that the IRA had just bombed Musgrave Park Hospital, killing two young soldiers. The newspapers also carried the report that the dead body of a young man was found in a car. Shortly before, the police had shot the car trying to scare off suspected joyriders. I found myself asking, "Has the world gone mad?"

The world, of course, has not gone mad. It is a world of the greatest beauty and perfection, marred only and being destroyed at an incredible rate by the human family's use and abuse. We know the world is dying, but we know too that with real determination and will we can save the world and turn it around. The only question is, Will we?

Humanity has not gone mad either. The deep warmth and capacity for real compassion among the people of Northern Ireland in the midst of war, the warmth and compassion of the Croat and Serb peoples in their war, and among all peoples, confuses and shocks the inquiring visitor. "I don't understand," we observe. "The people are so kind. How can this fighting go on?"

In their natural repulsion against cruelty and violence and in order to meet their need to find answers and make some sense out of nonsense, people everywhere often rush to blame someone, anyone but themselves, for evil. Their judgments are often dangerously simplistic: "It's the federal army, the Communists, the Provos, the loyalists, the British army, etc., etc." "Get rid of the men of violence and all will be well and we good people can get on with our lives." How often have we heard this phrase in Northern Ireland!

Yet we fail to recognize that we ourselves are part of the problem. Change will come about only when each one of us takes up the daily struggle to be more forgiving, more compassionate, more loving, and even more joyful in the knowledge that we ourselves, by some miracle of grace, can change, as those around us can change too. Therein lies our hope for a better future. So too, from this struggle within ourselves to be more truly human comes the truth that all life is sacred. Love is stronger than hate. We come to realize that this unseen force of love is acting throughout our world today in a mysterious way, helping humanity to come to a new understanding of life, and to a new refusal to take the gift of life from another human person.

The rebirth of humanity will not come without pain. The cry for life and the right to personal freedom continue to be ignored, ridiculed, or crushed with violence, war, and oppression by the state, whether in the former Yugoslavia or here, as it tries to impose its idea of "order." I never cease to be amazed at the government's demand for "order" instead of "justice."

Once we the people have given the state our permission to act on our behalf, once we have allowed the "lie" to take root that the state can uphold "order" even by taking human life, it doesn't matter then whether the price will be one life or a million lives, they will argue that they are only doing the job we pay them to do.

Somewhere, somehow, we have got things all wrong. We are all responsible. We all need to start again, to refuse the state's right to oppress and kill, to continue to cry out for life and justice, to give birth to a new world. We need to create societies where people in local communities learn to live together, acknowledging and celebrating their differences, without threatening or killing each other, without being held in a destructive cocoon of armed state protection and domination. Perhaps we can learn "community politics" where local people have a say in what happens in their own lives, in their own communities, thereby restoring their dignity, their sense of identity, and their importance to one another and the earth.

No, the world has not gone mad. I believe what we are seeing are butterflies bursting forth into freedom, shedding old ways, and looking for new life. Some butterflies get killed in this rebirth, as the young Chinese students in the pro-democracy movement, as the people in the struggling democracies in the Third World, and as the villagers in the former Yugoslavia have all died in their struggle for justice. But in the final analysis, the human species has taken wings. It is flying and it cannot be stopped.

In all this, the people of Northern Ireland can take great hope that here too there are many butterflies who want to fly to a new society, to help create a new humanity right here. While no one can take away the pain of those who have lost loved ones during the last decades, perhaps their pain can be eased knowing that if their suffering has helped birth a new humanity, then the pain has not been in vain.

Like millions of people, we want a world without killing and violence. It is true that the cost of stripping ourselves of the old ways and stepping onto the new path of nonviolence will not be without pain. But we can take courage and be strengthened in the knowledge that there are many of us traveling together and shaping this part of human history in this new way.

15

Japan's Mission of Peace

I would like to speak about my conviction that homicide, violence, cruelty, and war are counterproductive, immoral, and unacceptable. I believe therefore that it is of the utmost urgency for the future of humanity that we develop a new way of thinking and living based on the principle of absolute respect for human life and the environment.

Let us begin by looking at some examples of violence.

I am sure there is no better place on earth to speak about the immorality of war than here in Japan. We remember with shame the crime of North American Christians who dropped the atomic bomb on Hiroshima and Nagasaki in August 1945. Over two hundred thousand died and many more suffered and died later from the diseases caused by radiation. As a Christian, I repent of these crimes, and I ask the Japanese people to forgive us all for the cruelty and inhumanity committed against them. Each year, for forty days, concluding on the anniversary of Nagasaki's destruction, Christians in Ireland and North America fast and pray for our conversion to Christian nonviolence. Toward the end of our fast, we hold days of remembrance for the Hiroshima and Nagasaki martyrs.

We now know what the weapons of war can do to the world. The Japanese people have the moral authority to say to the world: "Abolish war. No country is allowed to use its weapons against another. No more war! Remove the roots of war, fear, and hatred, and uphold the physical, civil, and spiritual rights of all. Do not desire to dominate others. Do not even prepare for war!"

Some people will argue that it is impossible to abolish war because there is something in our biological make-up that is inherently violent. According to the Seville Statement on Violence, this myth is simply not true. This statement was prepared by twenty leading biological and social scientists and scholars from twelve nations and endorsed by the American Psychological Association and other research groups. The experts met in

A presentation to the Third Nobel Forum, in Tokyo, Japan, October 1990.

Seville, Spain, on May 16, 1986, to review the evidence for the
popular belief that war is natural.

"It is scientifically incorrect to say that we have inherited a
tendency to make war from our animal ancestors," the statement concludes. "Warfare is a peculiarly human phenomenon
and does not occur in other animals. . . . It is also incorrect to say
that war or other violent behavior is genetically programmed
into our human nature. While genes are involved at all levels
of the nervous system, they provide a developmental potential
that can be actualized only in conjunction with the ecologi-
cal and social environment." By showing how some nations
have moved toward peace and away from their violent histories, the Seville Statement argues that "the fact that warfare has
changed so radically over time indicates that it is a product of
culture. . . . War is biologically possible, but is not inevitable. . . .
The same species which invented war is capable of inventing
peace. The responsibility lies with each of us."

Of course, violence takes many different forms, including the repressive violence of the state and the revolutionary
violence of "the armed struggle," as in the case of my own
Northern Ireland.

We too know the immorality and pain of violence. In 1976,
the Peace People movement began, after the tragic deaths of
sixteen hundred people in the first seven years of the Troubles,
and the particular tragedy that killed my niece and nephews,
and eventually my sister. I mention this personal story because
it is the price of war. It is important we do not become immune
by talking about thousands of dead. We risk then losing sight of
the importance of each single life. One death from war is one
death too many.

Sadly, this Northern Irish tragedy continues. Northern Ireland's one and a half million people, from differing religious,
political, and cultural backgrounds, are unable to reject violence and create structures based on respect for human life,
equality, human rights, and inclusivity. In Northern Ireland,
there is a great deal of state injustice. The British government has removed many basic human rights. The restoration of
these human rights is a priority if the people are to move forward to dialogue, reconciliation, and justice. If the government
upholds human rights and participates in dialogue with all parties involved, then they will offer an alternative to "the armed

struggle." While we recognize the right of all to work for their political aspirations and to work to remove injustice, we must refuse the paramilitary forces the right to take life.

Still another level of violence that cripples our world is the violence of massive military spending by the First World nations, the violence of the enforced Third World debt, and the violence of environmental destruction. Surely, it is immoral that the First World spends two million dollars every minute of every day on militarism while nearly sixty thousand children die of starvation every day. Even in the First World, we find growing poverty, homelessness, and hunger. We have been told that military spending is necessary for our security. This is a lie. We cannot use these weapons without destroying millions of fellow human beings and causing unknown consequences to the environment. The Cold War is over. Let us all work to do whatever we can to encourage total disarmament and the transfer of our resources, scientific research, technology, and money to ending world hunger and poverty.

UNICEF reports that half a million children have died in the Third World because of the international debt crisis, and thousands more die each day. For these countries, poverty and misery get worse every day, not better. The poor are being strangled economically in a vain attempt to repay the debts from loans by foreign banks now totaling over 1.3 trillion dollars.

"The debt crisis could be made an instrument of hope and liberation, not oppression and despair," writes Dr. Susan George, an American economist. "If we have the courage to write off the debt we could demand in return that the debtor government make payments in local currency into national department funds. These funds would be used for development projects and for environmental renewal. We must get the money and the power that goes with it to those who have never had either. The people and the planet have paid more than enough."

Part of the violence of environmental destruction is the huge deforestation around the planet. In Malaysia, deforestation destroys the homes of the Penan Forest people. When they tried to stop deforestation, they were threatened or imprisoned. They received no support from the government. I mention this tragedy because the lumbering companies export this wood to Japan. I believe that the Japanese people would be distressed to realize what is happening and would want to help the Penan tribes to save their forest.

These tropical forests sustain the climates, and each of us must do all we can to stop their destruction. Deforestation is linked to the debt crisis. Unless countries which hold the vast amount of rain forests receive serious debt relief in the next few years, there is no chance of saving the tropical rain forests.

There is great concern too among many people that Japan should stop its policy of whaling. If future generations are to enjoy these beautiful creatures, we need to do everything we can to protect them now.

I do not need to speak further about the multiple dimensions of violence, both personal, interpersonal, national and international. What we need is the will to put into practice the only alternative before us: active nonviolence. By nonviolence I mean stopping every form of violence, from cruelty to murder to war. Nonviolence does not mean that we allow evil to run rampant; rather, nonviolence demands action and creativity to resist evil. I believe that hope for the future depends on each of us taking nonviolence into our hearts and minds and developing new and imaginative structures which are nonviolent and life-giving for all.

Some people will argue that this is too idealistic. I believe it is very realistic. I am convinced that humanity is fast evolving to this higher consciousness. For those who say it cannot be done, let us remember that humanity learned to abolish slavery. Our task now is no less than the abolition of violence and war.

As I was reflecting on this speech, I asked myself what was the most important thing to say to the Japanese people. As you know, I am a Christian. So I went into a church and asked the Lord Jesus what he wanted me to tell you. The message I received was, "Tell the people to stop killing each other."

How can this be, I thought, unless people learn to respect human life. A short time later, I read the following statement by your own scientist, poet, and mystic, Dr. Takashi Nagai of Nagasaki: "Precisely because we Japanese had treated human life so simply and so carelessly, precisely for this reason we were reduced to our present miserable plight. Respect for the life of every person, this must be the foundation stone on which we would build a new society."

In the English translation of Dr. Nagai's sorrowful and powerful book, *The Bells of Nagasaki,* Fr. William Johnston, S.J., describes this great spirit as a "mystic of peace in our times." Young people seeking truth used to travel to visit Dr. Nagai in his house, which he called Nyokodo ("The love your neighbor as yourself house"). Listen to the advice he gave them: "Go to the mountains and meditate! If you stay in the hurly-burly of this world, you'll run around in circles without ever finding your way. But the blue mountains are immovable and the white clouds come and go. I look constantly at the mountains of Mitsuyama and continue my meditation."

During my visit to the cities of Hiroshima and Nagasaki, I thought that one cannot but admire and congratulate the Japanese people on the way in which they have rebuilt their lives and cities out of such suffering and devastation. Their example of courage, perseverance, and achievement is indeed an inspiration to us in Northern Ireland. I found my visits to the peace memorials painful and felt moved to repentance, but I celebrate with the people their vision of a more peaceful world to which these two cities have dedicated themselves.

It was a great privilege for me to visit the home of Dr. Nagai in Nagasaki. Through his meditation and personal suffering and the suffering of the Japanese people, Dr. Nagai found a great truth. He came to know that "loving our neighbors as we love ourselves" is the only way to world peace. Dr. Nagai knew that as killing starts in the heart, so too does nonviolence. All of us must therefore make our own pilgrimage to peace. This pilgrimage is unique. It must go in two directions. One roads leads inward to the depths of our being; the other road leads outward to our fellow human beings and the universe. For many the inner road is less known and less traveled.

Perhaps the reason why many do not travel the inner road is that they refuse to recognize our own dark shadow, our own evil lurking within. We think the root of the problem is the violence of other people or the greed of other nations. We refuse to see the root cause as our own selves. We maintain that we are not violent and that we could not kill. The reality is that under certain circumstances, we are all capable of evil. If we allow selfishness, greed, and hate to take root in our hearts, their fruits will be cruelty, violence, and often homicide and war. The hard work of nonviolence begins within our own conscience, as Dr. Nagai knew. It is here that we find the spirit of love and truth. Our inner pilgrimage can lead us to the knowledge of our true selves. Then we realize that we are one with all people and with the universe.

I cannot give you a blueprint for this inner journey. Each of us must walk our own path in the way best suited for us. However, I am happy to be here in Japan, because I know that you in the East have much to teach us in the West, as we walk together in spirit, along our pilgrimages to the truth of peace.

What I can do though is share with you some things which I have come to accept as truths for me in my own life. First, let me confess that I know nothing. I have little education. With every passing day, I realize more deeply how incomprehensible life really is, how little I know about the wonderful mystery of our being and the universe. In the words of your own man of peace, Dr. Kagawa, "In the depths of my soul, I am daily conscious of the miracle of creation." My life, all life, is full of uncertainty, too. There are, however, some things of which I am certain. I am certain that God is, Love is, human life is sacred, and that I exist and that I will die.

For a long time, I took my life for granted. Then I came to know with a deep sense of knowing that I have been given the gift of life by God. It is a gift that should be celebrated and re-joiced in and shared with others in loving service. I came to see that I have a right to my life and no one has a right to take it from me. So if I ask natural justice from my fellow travelers in respecting my right to life, then I too must give justice and re-spect their right to life. This means that I can never kill another human person.

During the height of the Troubles in Belfast, I remember witnessing injustice and wondering if it was right to take up arms against institutional violence and state injustice. In church, kneeling before a crucifix of Jesus, I heard the message, "Thou shalt not kill. Love one another as I have loved you." I knew then that while I must have the deepest compassion and respect for all people who use violence against evil, I must be clearly convinced that it is not the Christian way. The way of Jesus Christ is the way of active nonviolence against evil. He does not use evil means to fight evil. As a Christian, I repent that we Christians have not taught or lived the full gospel message of Jesus' nonviolence and love for enemies. I am convinced, however, that we are evolving into a new age, and that in time, the Christian church will again proclaim a theology of nonviolence as the norm for Christian life.

Together with nonviolence, it is important that we undertake the work of repentance, forgiveness, and reconciliation around the world. Through the repentance, forgiveness, and reconciliation of the world's nations, we can find hope for humanity's future. With a policy of reconciliation between old rival countries, we can make a new future and not just relive an old past.

Around our world, societies are based on structures upheld by violent institutions. Most countries have large armies. What is needed is a living example of people building their societies on the principle of respect for human life and all creation. Japan is to be congratulated for its decision not to have an army. In this respect, you have an important mission to the world. Can you be a witness to the world not only that countries do not need an army, but that government structures can be built on respect for all human life?

In time, we hope, other countries may follow your example and disarm. I have a dream that Ireland too, now a neutral country with a small army, will someday disarm completely and also be a light to a troubled world. Germany too may well offer great hope to the world if in the future its people decide on neutrality and disarmament. We can rejoice and celebrate today because we are living in a miraculous time. Everything is changing and everything is possible.

Finally, I would like to thank the Japanese people for their message of peace proclaimed so faithfully to the world for so many years now. You have given hope and inspiration to those of us struggling for peace in our own situations. It is because of this faithfulness to peace that I make one request to the Japanese people. You have renounced war. You have no army. I beg you never rearm. Never let the wealthy nations force you into purchasing arms. May Japan be a beacon of nonviolence and peace to the whole world.

16

In Memory of Ken Saro Wiwa

I had the great pleasure to meet Ken Saro Wiwa at a peace conference in Holland in 1994. He told me about the struggle of his people in Ogoniland, Nigeria, to save the environment and how much his people were suffering. He said they were engaged in a nonviolent struggle and he had great hope for the future of his country because of the spirit of the Ogoni people.

He told us then that he had come to Europe to appeal to the international community for help to save the Ogoni people. Sadly, it took too long for the international community to wake up to the cry for justice and environmental rights for the half million Ogoni people against the giants of Shell Oil Company and the Nigerian military regime.

The oil company and the military tried in many ways to silence this peaceful man, but Ken would not be silenced. He spoke the truth and began to stir the conscience of millions of people around the world. He became too much of a threat to the giants.

In a vain attempt to silence the truth, Ken and eight others were convicted of a crime they did not commit and put in prison. They suffered sixty-five days in chains, weeks of starvation, and months of mental torture. Finally, they were subjected to a kangaroo court, dubbed "a special military tribunal," which sentenced them to death.

Today, we remember our dear friends Ken Saro Wiwa and the eight other Ogoni men, executed one year ago on November 10, 1995, by the Nigerian government. The only crime these nine men committed was to love their people enough to call for a restoration of full human and environmental rights. They protested the destruction of their homes and the very air they need to breathe by the world's largest petrol company, Shell Oil. They protested the brutality, torture, and killings of their people by the Nigerian military regime. For this they were tortured and executed.

A reflection offered on the first anniversary of the execution of nonviolent activist Ken Saro Wiwa and eight other Ogoni activists by the Nigerian government, at a vigil and protest outside a Shell gas station in Belfast.

Ken's last words on the gallows were: "Lord, take my soul. The struggle goes on."

Today, we continue the struggle by joining with the Ogoni people. We remember what Ken wrote from his prison cell: "I have one suggestion for those whose conscience has been disturbed by my story. Boycott all Shell products. Picket Shell garages and mechanics. Do not allow them to profit by their destruction of the people and ecology of the Niger Delta. Help us in our struggle for justice and human rights in Nigeria."

But Shell is not the only corporation responsible for the destruction of Ogoniland and the death of its people. In a letter from his prison bed to the *Guardian* on Thursday, May 18, 1995, Ken wrote: "Ultimately the fault lies at the door of the British government. It is the British government which supplies arms and credit to the military dictators of Nigeria, knowing full well that all such weapons will be used only against innocent, unarmed citizens. It is the British government which makes noises about democracy in Nigeria and Africa but supports military dictators to the hilt. It is the British government which supports the rape and devastation of the environment by a valued tax-paying, laboring-employing organization like Shell. I lay my travails, the destruction of the Ogoni and other peoples in the Niger Delta, at the door of the British government. Ultimately, the decision is for the British people to stop this grand deceit, this double standard, which has lengthened the African nightmare and denigrates humanity."

Today, we honor the memory of Ken and his friends and commit ourselves to carry on Ken's work. We come to this Shell gas station to protest against the destruction of the Ogoni people and the Niger Delta. We call for the immediate release of all political prisoners, the release of the bodies of the nine men killed one year ago, the immediate withdrawal of all troops in the Niger Delta, a worldwide ban on the sale of weapons to Nigeria, freedom of speech and assembly in Nigeria, an international embargo on all Nigerian oil and gas products, and full democracy in Nigeria and compensation from the oil company to the people.

We remember Ken's last words, "The struggle goes on." In his memory and in support of the Nigerian people, we join their struggle.

17

Freedom for East Timor

There are many of us who like to think that as we move into the twenty-first century we are becoming more civilized and enlightened. We use terms like "the global village" and "interconnectedness." We surf the net and see the great political and social changes in our world. Yet since 1975, East Timor has suffered under Indonesia's brutal military occupation. And so we ask the question, "How is it possible in this interdependent, interconnected world, for an illegal occupation and genocide to continue unabated for so long?"

In East Timor, one-third of the population, over two hundred thousand people, have died at the hands of the Indonesian military. Over forty thousand Indonesian troops now control a population of just eight hundred thousand people. On November 12, 1991, the Indonesian military fired on thousands of unarmed, peaceful demonstrators at the Santa Cruz cemetery in Dili, killing more than 250 people. The Indonesian occupiers carry out a policy of forced sterilization on the Timorese women. Their encouragement of transmigration of Indonesians has adversely affected the East Timorese. In short, with the support of Britain and the United States, the Indonesian government practices genocide against the East Timorese.

The international community has the ability to stop this slaughter. All that is necessary is the political will. The international community must affirm that the Indonesian invasion and occupation of East Timor constitute blatant and gross violations of international law of self-determination and human rights. I encourage the European Union to monitor the human rights and support the self-determination of the East Timorese people, to halt all military aid, sales, and assistance to Indonesia, and to refuse to recognize Indonesia's annexation of East Timor.

It is particularly important that the First World halt all military assistance and arms sales to Indonesia. The export of Hawk fighter jets and other arms from Britain continues, but not un-

Previously unpublished, written in the spring of 1998.

challenged. In July 1996, four women, the "Seeds of Hope Plowshares," were acquitted of all charges by a jury after they hammered on a Hawk jet destined for Indonesia at British Aerospace. Their willingness to undergo prison and risk heavy financial penalties and their stunning court victory against British Aerospace gives us hope to carry on our efforts to stop all weapons sales to Indonesia and to pursue total disarmament.

In Belfast, we too must take responsibility for the provision of military hardware. We often hear in our media about the bomb factories of the IRA and the loyalist paramilitaries and rightly so, but seldom do we acknowledge the presence of Shorts, the biggest missile-making factory right in our midst here in Belfast. Although most of Shorts's products are in the civilian sector, including parts to airlines and small jets, their missile division produces several types of short-range surface-to-air missiles. On a U.K. list of military equipment sold to Indonesia, the name of Shorts appears: "Shorts Brothers sold 96 Seacat ship-to-air and ship-to-ship air missile launchers. The contract was signed in 1986 and deliveries took place between 1986 and 1988."

The fact that these Shorts missiles are now in the possession of the Indonesian military, which came to power after the death of about one million Indonesian people, is of concern to us all. It is of the utmost importance that we all take responsibility for what we produce and how these products are used in our name.

Hitler's Germany could have been different had individuals taken responsibility for the government's actions and resisted them. In his book *Conjectures of a Guilty Bystander,* Thomas Merton quotes the following letter written by L. A. Topf and Sons, manufacturers of heating equipment, to the commandant of Auschwitz, concerning a new heating system: "We acknowledge the receipt of your order for five triple furnaces, including two electric elevators for raising the corpses and one emergency elevator. For putting the bodies into the furnace, we suggest simply a metal fork moving on cylinder. For transporting the corpses, we suggest using light carts on wheels. We are submitting plans for our perfected cremation ovens, which operate with coal and have hitherto given you full satisfaction. We guarantee their effectiveness as well as their durability."

Hitler was only one man. He required thousands of other

people to help him commit genocide against six million Jews and others. Each of us needs to search our conscience and ask if our lives and work contribute to enriching and beautifying life or supporting death and destruction for our fellow human beings.

If people in Northern Ireland can persuade Shorts to re-direct all its efforts to nonmilitary products, this could offer an example to other producers of military equipment in other countries. Such a move by Shorts would give hope and encouragement to the peoples of the Third World who cry out to Western governments to stop sending weapons and instead to send food, medicine, and educational supplies for their children. I encourage individuals involved in the production of weapons to resign and seek employment in more life-enhancing work.

In a visit last year to Belfast, Nobel Peace Prize winner Bishop Belo of East Timor said that there will not be a military solution to the Indonesian/East Timor situation. It can be solved only through dialogue and negotiation. We in Northern Ireland understand. From our own personal experience we know that our own ethnic/political problems can be solved only if all parties in the conflict listen to each other and work together nonviolently for a solution. I support the proposal that the European Union call for the immediate and unconditional release of the East Timorese leader Xanana Gusmao, to enable him to participate in the ongoing UN-sponsored talks. We take hope from the growing movement of Indonesians calling for human rights and democracy within Indonesia and also for East Timor. We know how high a price Indonesian activists often pay for raising their voices. We salute and applaud their courage.

Despite these many years of occupation and the horrendous human rights violations, we see signs of hope for East Timor. By awarding the Nobel Peace Prize to Bishop Belo and José Ramos Horta (East Timor's foreign minister in exile), the international community recognizes the suffering of the East Timorese people and their long struggle for human rights and democracy. The fall of Indonesia's dictator Suharto in the spring of 1998 may also pave the way for a free East Timor. But the world needs to continue to pressure Indonesia.

We know that the task of building a genuine, nonviolent

democracy in East Timor, Indonesia, Northern Ireland, and everywhere is a lifelong commitment. When we all join in solidarity and surrender to this enormous challenge, the fruits of joy and peace, friendship and love become God's gift to us and our gift to each other. Together we carry on the struggle and know that freedom for East Timor and for us all will be granted one day soon.

18

Fr. Zabelka, Hiroshima, and Our Conversion to Peace

Fr. George Zabelka died on April 11, 1992, in Flint, Michigan. He was seventy-seven years old and had spent the latter part of his life as a reluctant prophet, traveling around the world, teaching and preaching the way of active nonviolence.

I first met Fr. George when he came to Belfast in 1988 to join Fr. Charlie McCarthy and others in a forty-day fast for the church's conversion to the truth of Christian nonviolence.

This was Fr. George's second visit to Ireland. In 1982–83, at the age of sixty-seven, Fr. George walked seventy-five hundred miles from the Trident nuclear submarine base in Bangor, Washington, to Bethlehem, Israel, traveling through Ireland en route. Some of those who participated in the peace walk remember that Fr. George had written the name "Hiroshima" and the name "Nagasaki" on each shoe. His walk was a pilgrimage of repentance for the crimes of Hiroshima and Nagasaki.

Fr. Zabelka did not always feel this way. In 1945, he was a Catholic U.S. army chaplain on the island of Tinian in the South Pacific. He served as a Catholic chaplain for the personnel of the 509th Composite Group, the atomic bomb team. He offered Mass and other services for them on Sundays and weekdays. He literally blessed their mission of atomic destruction. During his tour of duty on Tinian island, he was very much in the military mind-set, convinced that not only the atomic bombing but also the indiscriminate fire bombing of Japanese cities was morally justified. He was assigned to serve occupied Japan in October 1945, and visited both Hiroshima and Nagasaki, not only the devastated areas, but also the survivors at medical centers. Returning to the United States in December 1946, he was discharged, joined the Michigan National Guard, and returned to the normal duties of a parish priest.

Previously unpublished, written in the spring of 1992.

His conversion to peacemaking began when he visited the medical centers around Hiroshima and Nagasaki and saw the burned, disfigured faces of the women and children, the innocent victims. For twenty-five years after the war, he struggled with that experience, agonizing because he knew that the alleged just war theory strictly prohibits the harming of innocent civilians.

In the early 1960s, Fr. George worked in conjunction with Martin Luther King, Jr., during the civil rights struggle and was deeply inspired by the example and words of nonviolent action. For the first time, he was brought face to face with Christian nonviolent resistance to evil. Fr. Zabelka later wrote about this period: "I recall King's words after being jailed in Montgomery, Alabama. King said, 'Blood may flow in the streets of Montgomery before we receive our freedom, but it must be our blood that flows, and not that of the white man. We must not harm a single hair on the head of our white brothers.'" Fr. Zabelka added, "I struggled, argued, but realized, yes, it was there in the Sermon on the Mount, 'Love your enemies, return good for evil.'"

In 1973, Fr. George attended a retreat on Christian nonviolence led by Fr. Charlie McCarthy. This retreat marked a turning point in his life. Two years later, he wrote to his friends announcing that he had reached the conclusion that Jesus taught a way of nonviolent love toward friends and enemies, and that "therefore, I must do an about face!"

For a man who was nicknamed "General George" and who was once reprimanded in the military for "excessive zeal," this about face was like the conversion of Saul.

"I went through a crisis of faith," Fr. Zabelka told Fr. McCarthy. "I'm a practical man and those words of Jesus, 'Love your enemies, do good to those who hate you, turn the other cheek when someone strikes you,' were completely impractical. Impractical and unworkable. I couldn't understand it. In many ways, I still don't. Yet Jesus took this course of suffering and nonviolence. His words were so clear, and so is the example of his life and death. For me, the issue was very simple. Either Jesus was God or he wasn't. If not, then his words could be dismissed as idealism. But if he was God, then he meant what he said. He wasn't kidding. He could not be dismissed as an idealist who didn't understand human reality. So either I accept what he says as coming from God or else I forget about the whole business, forget about Christianity entirely. My crisis was a practical one. My choice was made on the basis of faith."

After his conversion to the way of nonviolence, Fr. George spent every minute of his life praying, working, speaking, and walking for peace. He called the universal church — Catholics, Protestants, and Orthodox — "to stop making war respectable." In 1984, he made a pilgrimage to Hiroshima and Nagasaki, where he said, "I was wrong; I am sorry," to the Hibakushas (the atomic bomb survivors). He challenged the churches to preach Christ's teachings of nonviolent love and mercy and to repent publicly for their failure and the failure of their predecessors to teach explicitly this message of love and mercy and no to killing.

It may be argued that what he asked the churches to do is impossible, but who would have believed that the tough "General George," who spent his adulthood blessing war, could turn into such a gentle giant.

These thoughts came to me during my last lovely evening spent in Fr. Zabelka's company. He was happy and joyous on that occasion and took great delight in telling me about finding a little spider in his room, cupping her in his hands, and putting her in his cupboard to be warm and safe. When I told this story to my son, John, he said, "It would be heaven if everyone was like that."

Perhaps Fr. Zabelka had come to know this truth, and that is why he spent the latter part of his earthly life giving out tens of thousands of buttons which said, "Do Something for Peace." His life was an inspiration and a testimony to the truth that we can change and we can all "do something for peace." To those who had the pleasure of meeting him on his pilgrimage of peace around the world, he will long be remembered as "the gentle prophet."

19

Daniel and Philip Berrigan, Brothers against War

In December 1997, I nominated Daniel and Philip Berrigan for the Nobel Peace Prize. These two brothers are the most prominent faith-based voices for peace and nonviolence in the United States.

I nominated these two peacemaking men because for many years I have been inspired by their courageous actions against war and nuclear madness. They follow in the footsteps of an American woman for whom I had great admiration — Dorothy Day. As a young member working in the Legion of Mary in Andersonstown, Belfast, I sometimes helped in Regina Coeli Hostel for destitute women. Through this work, I learned about the work of Dorothy Day, founder of the Catholic Worker movement, which offers hospitality to the homeless and works for justice and peace. Dorothy was born one hundred years ago and died in 1980.

In 1977, I visited the Catholic Worker houses in New York City and met Dorothy. She lived in a little room in Mary's House, sharing the poverty of New York's homeless women. I was shocked by the extreme poverty and the sheer numbers of the homeless. I have visited the United States many times and each time continue to be shocked by the poverty I see in all the states I have visited.

I love America, but I long for the day when the American people will raise their voices together and demand that their government stops squandering billions of their tax money on weapons of war and instead diverts it to feeding the hungry and housing the homeless.

Dorothy Day was a true prophet of nonviolence, and even in death her voice is heard. She challenges her government to convert its huge military budget toward feeding the hungry and solving its growing social problems. Prophets arise in every

Published in the *Irish News*, January 8, 1998.

generation to speak truth to those in power and their voices are heard no matter how hard the authorities try to silence them.

Daniel and Philip Berrigan are such prophetic voices.

Philip is a seventy-four-year-old former Josephite priest, the father of three children, and co-founder of Jonah House, a peace community in Baltimore. He is currently serving a three-year prison sentence in a federal prison in Petersburg, Virginia, for an antinuclear demonstration.

Together with his brother, Fr. Daniel Berrigan, a seventy-seven-year-old Jesuit priest, poet, and author of over forty books, who was a close friend of Dorothy Day and Thomas Merton, he has consistently spoken out for peace, justice, and disarmament. During their lifetimes, the Berrigans have inspired many people through their nonviolent civil disobedience actions against war and injustice. They have taken onto themselves much suffering but always refuse to inflict pain or suffering on others, as they act for peace and justice.

On May 17, 1968, Philip and Daniel Berrigan were arrested with seven others in Catonsville, Maryland, for burning U.S. draft files with homemade napalm in opposition to the Vietnam war. The Catonsville Nine action attracted international attention and sparked hundreds of similar actions. Millions of people joined in the public outcry against the war because of their courageous witness. Daniel Berrigan served two years in prison for this action, and nearly died while in prison. He was released in 1972. Philip Berrigan served two and half years in prison.

On September 9, 1980, Philip and Daniel Berrigan and six others entered the General Electric nuclear manufacturing plant in King of Prussia, Pennsylvania, and hammered on unarmed nuclear nosecones, thereby symbolically "beating swords into plowshares," following the biblical vision of the prophet Isaiah. Their ten-year prison sentence was appealed and overturned in 1990.

Both Daniel and Philip have each been arrested over one hundred times in peaceful, prayerful acts of civil disobedience against preparation for war. On February 12, 1997, Phil boarded a U.S. nuclear-capable Navy destroyer at the Bath Iron Works in Maine, and with five others hammered on unarmed weapons, once again calling for total nuclear disarmament and the abolition of war. When he finishes his current two-year sentence, he will have spent ten years of his life behind bars for peace.

We are all indebted to Daniel and Philip Berrigan for their efforts on all our behalf. They continue to attract widespread media interest, to influence religion and politics, and to inspire countless people around the world.

From his jail cell in Maine, Philip Berrigan wrote in November 1997: "We will not abolish nuclear weapons, not win representation in government, not reduce the staggering gap between rich and poor, not stop the occupation of the United States by military and corporate elites, until we learn again to say No! How much time will God allow us to end this mad march toward death and the destruction of the planet? We have already had over fifty years. Only an act of God, working through the sacrifices of thousands of valiant people, has forestalled nuclear war. But the danger is still imminent. Moreover, the planet is profoundly poisoned and becomes more so as we delay. We pray with you from prison that you offer a resounding No! to the curse of war, nuclear and interventionary. So help us God."

In nominating Phil and Dan Berrigan for the Nobel Peace Prize, I feel privileged to add my voice to theirs in saying No! to death and Yes! to peace and life, both here in the United States and around the world.

20

One Night in a U.S. Jail

On Monday, February 16, 1998, I visited Philip Berrigan in the Petersburg federal prison, near Richmond, Virginia. It was the first time I had met Phil. I went to visit him to join in solidarity for his work for peace and disarmament. Seventy-four-year-old Phil Berrigan was serving a two-year prison sentence for an antinuclear Plowshares demonstration on Ash Wednesday, 1997, at the Bath Iron Works in Maine. Together with his brother Daniel, he has been arrested repeatedly in prayerful acts of civil disobedience for the cause of peace and disarmament.

Before visiting Phil, I had spent some of the previous week campaigning in Belfast against the massive U.S.-British military bombings of Iraq, which were imminent, and against U.S. sanctions on Iraq, which have caused the death of at least six Iraqi children per hour since the 1991 Gulf war.

During the drive out to the Petersburg prison, I told a Catholic Worker friend that I intended to carry out civil disobedience by refusing to leave the prison in protest against both a military strike by the United States and Britain and the U.S. sanctions. I wanted also to protest U.S. war preparations and ongoing U.S. nuclear weapons policy. I asked him to phone my husband, Jackie, and Peace People friends, after my arrest and detention. Before leaving Belfast, I had already discussed my possible action with Jackie.

That morning, I had a three-hour visit with Phil. He looked fit and healthy. His wife, Elizabeth, family, and friends were very much in his conversation, and I knew that their love and support gave him strength and courage to do what he was doing.

I told him I wanted to carry out civil disobedience by refusing to leave the prison, thereby risking arrest. I said I would not do this without his permission as I was deeply conscious of the repercussions against him. Phil was surprised by my decision to take this action. He told me I must act according to my own conscience, thereby leaving the decision entirely up to me. He

Previously unpublished.

said they would probably question him, but that he would be all right. He said that it is good to pray and fast, but these should prepare us for nonviolent action and civil disobedience.

Halfway through our visit, the prison guards called all the prisoners to line up. I watched Phil join one of the lines of inmates and stand to be counted. While watching Philip Berrigan in the line-up, I finally made up my mind to "go to jail" and join him and his colleagues in "standing up to be counted."

I remembered that Gandhi, King, and Dorothy Day urged people to "fill the jails" in opposition to war and injustice. Prison was only a little sacrifice to endure in the face of such terrible suffering the poor live under, while our governments squander billions of dollars on weapons of mass destruction (fifteen thousand nuclear weapons in the U.S. alone). At noon, we prayed for each other, for Elizabeth and Jackie, our families and friends, for everyone. Finally, we said goodbye, and Philip stood up. He continued to wave and smile at me. I approached the guard and explained I would not be leaving the prison and why.

The rest of the day was spent between prison officials and FBI agents questioning me and threatening me with all sorts of calamities if I continued to refuse to leave the prison. Finally, that evening, I was arrested for trespassing on federal property, taken to the Richmond city jail, and informed that I would go to court the following morning.

In jail, I was forced by a rubber-gloved officer to strip and put on a yellow jail suit. Everything was taken from me, and I was led to a solitary cell in a block of four cell units. Solitary was not at all what I had expected. It was desperately noisy. The three inmates on my block could not see each other, so they yelled and cursed at the top of their voices across the block to one another. One cried and moaned like a wounded animal, while another kept threatening to beat and kill her. (I learned later that one of the young women had murdered her baby.) Another inmate kept moaning that she was glad to be in the cell and safe from the men who beat her.

For many hours, the doors slammed, keys jangled, the radio blasted, and the inmates continued their cursing and threatening each other. I found it impossible to sleep. I had to choose whether to go to court quietly the following morning, or to remain in jail — and refuse to go. I felt if I remained in jail as long as possible it would bring more attention to the issues and help those outside campaigning for peace, but if I went to court immediately the authorities might well dismiss me in order to keep my protest as quiet as possible. This indecision was painful and tough. I prayed for guidance.

Finally I decided I would refuse to leave the cell and try to remain there as long as possible. I felt a deep peaceful presence. I experienced joy and, in spite of the prison bars, even a sense of personal freedom.

Later that morning, after I refused to leave several times, three female guards pushed me down on the bed, forcibly dressed me, put my arm up my back almost breaking it, and ran me down several flights of stairs. They shoved me into a holding cell. A dozen inmates were waiting there to go to court. The women were being held on charges ranging from drug possession to prostitution to theft. They were young and of different ethnic backgrounds.

I will never forget my short stay in that tiny, dirty, cramped, holding cell. Too many bodies, too much human suffering, all etched out on the face of each woman as each waited in fear and anger to be handcuffed and led away to court. I felt deeply sad and powerless in the midst of so much suffering. Up until then, I did not feel afraid, even when I was forcibly dressed and physically mistreated. However, because of the close confinement and the long wait, tension among the women began to rise and some of them began to shout and abuse each other. I was sure it was only a matter of time before a fight broke out, and I knew that I was getting anxious and deeply conscious of the threatening burly guards with their batons and guns just outside the cell door.

It is incredible to think that one and a half million people, the entire population of Northern Ireland, are in American prisons and jails. The whole system is geared to dehumanize, control, and weaken fellow human beings. Prison does not solve any problem. I wonder when the world's governments will begin to fight crime at its roots by ensuring justice for the poor.

Later that morning I was handcuffed and taken by an FBI agent to the federal court. Upon arrival, I was fingerprinted, photographed, and interviewed. I was held in a cell until 2:30 in the afternoon, when I was brought before Judge Williams.

I said I would not be asking anyone to put up bail, that I would defend myself, that I acknowledged that I had broken the law, and that I accepted whatever punishment was ordered. A hearing was set for 4:30 that afternoon.

In the meantime, I was allowed to leave with some of the local peace activists who had come to the court to support me. They explained how much personal suffering was involved for those who dared defy and challenge military policies. They told me, for example, about Steve Baggerly, a young Catholic Worker and father who was one of the six Prince of Peace Plowshares activists along with Phil. Although Phil and the others were serving longer sentences, Steve was released from prison on February 1, 1998, after serving one year in prison. He runs a small Catholic Worker house of hospitality for the homeless in Norfolk, Virginia, along with his wife, Kim Williams. When he was released from prison, the judge ordered that he could not return to his home and family and work for the poor in Virginia. Instead, he has to stay some eight hundred miles north in Maine — for the next three years! This internal exile bears many similarities to the worst of the old Soviet Russian suppression, when people were exiled to Siberia.

When he returned to court for the hearing, the prosecutor asked for the case to be dismissed. Judge Williams dismissed it. I asked if I could address the court. I said that I had indeed refused to leave the prison and accepted arrest, in order to protest the U.S. sanctions against Iraq and the death of six Iraqi children every hour and 1.2 million Iraqi people as a direct result of these sanctions. The judge interrupted me and pointed out that Saddam Hussein could stop this himself. I replied that he was not a good leader and didn't care for human rights and the children, but that we should not punish innocent children by policies that are both failed and immoral. I tried to go on to make the point against a U.S. military strike against Iraq and to protest U.S. war preparations and ongoing U.S. nuclear weapons policy, but he did not allow time for me to do so. Instead, he interrupted me to say that he knew of the Berrigan brothers, and that the next time I visited someone in jail, I was to leave when my visiting time was up.

After my night in jail and learning how others were treated, I was surprised that the case was completely dismissed. I thought there would be some kind of punishment and was willing to accept it. I was conscious of the contrast between Phil Berrigan serving several years in prison for civil disobedience and myself walking free with no punishment.

After returning home I learned that Phil Berrigan was punished for my actions. After he was questioned, he was placed in solitary confinement for ten days. Then, in mid-March, the regional supervisor of prisons issued an order preventing any further visits to Philip Berrigan for one year. This was unjust and draconian punishment. Since my action was solely my own decision and Phil Berrigan had not suggested it or talked me into it, then why was he punished for something I did? I find it unbelievable and unacceptable that Phil Berrigan's wife, children, and friends were also punished because of my action. I am appalled that the United States, which prides itself and presents itself to the world as the model of democracy, should so unjustly remove such a basic right as all visitations to a prisoner, in this case, to such a noble, nonviolent person as Phil Berrigan. This cruel and barbaric treatment of Phil is not acceptable behavior for any democratic country.

After several months of campaigning, Phil was allowed to see his wife, children, and friends, beginning in the summer of 1998. He was released from prison in November 1998 and along with his brother Dan will continue to speak out against war and nuclear weapons.

Philip Berrigan stands in the tradition of Mahatma Gandhi and Martin Luther King, Jr. He is one of the century's great voices for peace.

III

Peace for All Humanity

With school children at the Peace Park in Hiroshima.

21

A Peaceful Planet, Every Child's Birthright

There is nothing like the smile of a newborn baby to bring out the best in each of us. My mother always says that when a baby first smiles, it is because the baby sees the angels. True or not, the baby's magical smile can bring out the angel in all of us. It is not only the doting parents who want to give the child all the love and good things it needs. We all want to cuddle, love, and wish the best for this little gift of life from God. We know the most important thing for the baby is to be loved and to love. We know too the child needs to live in an atmosphere of peace in its own home, peace in its community, peace in its wider home, the planet earth.

Some children are lucky and find this peace. Sadly, a great many of earth's children experience only loneliness, pain, and violence. They quickly come to realize the reality of the world they have inherited. It is not a peaceful world.

It is a world steeped in cruelty, poverty, violence, homicide, and war. A world of injustice, pain, and loneliness where love is hard to find. A world where children are silently dying of starvation because of Third World debts (which could be written off). A world where governments spend $2 million every minute, every day, on militarism, while an ever-growing number of their own citizens go hungry, sleep in cardboard boxes, and die lonely, mercilessly stripped of all dignity and hope. A world where we use up and destroy our natural resources, such as the rain forests and water supply, a world that might be uninhabitable for future children. A world built on unjust and violent structures where human rights are ignored. A world where many children are daily subjected to the psychological causes of violence.

Dr. Joseph Cassius, a psychologist from Memphis, lists some of these psychological factors. First, we observe how our parents deal with each other. That's called modeling. If we observe

---

An address to the Pax Christi Assembly, Buffalo, New York, August 3, 1990.

our parents acting violently, that teaches us that the way to resolve conflict is by hitting, yelling, or some other aggressive
behavior.

Second, if we are abused personally by parents or parental
surrogates with verbal or physical violence or by abandonment
or the withholding of affection, this may hurt us to such a degree that we learn to hate ourselves and hate the one who hurts
us. We may begin to believe the negative verbal attributions or
at least to rebel against them.

Third, television and movies are marketed to our innocent
children with scenes of violence, sexual abuse, beatings, shooting, and other horrible behavior of one person against another.
Constant watching of the scene may be exciting to a child but
eventually may cause a numbing or deadening effect. The child
in each of us that is constantly exposed to aggressive and hos-
tile images may become callous to the pain and suffering one
person can cause another.

Dr. Cassius also notes that years of research suggest that lack
of affection and stroking breeds violence in children.

It would take a long time to examine all the multiple dimensions of violence which children have to face — personally,
interpersonally, internationally, and environmentally. Let me
just quote Vera Brittain: "If I write any more I shall probably
cry...which must never be done, for there is so much to cry
for here, that one might weep forever and yet not shed enough
tears to wipe away the pitiableness of it all."

In my own Northern Ireland, we too know the "pitiableness
of it all." Here too children continue to suffer, and some have
died unnecessarily because of the ongoing violence.

My sister Anne's three children died as a result of a British army chase of two young men. During the chase, one of
them was shot through the head and died instantly at the wheel
of the car, which then plowed into my niece and nephews on
the footpath. The following morning, August 11, 1976, I
walked around the hospital in Belfast with my brother-in-law,
Jackie Maguire. We went to see his son John (two and a half).
The doctor said John was dying. We went to see his daughter,
Joanne (eight), and his son Andrew (six weeks old) lying beside
each other dead. We went to see his wife, Anne. The doctor
said it would be a miracle if she lived. As we walked away,
Jackie said, "My three children dead, my darling Anne dying,

oh, how will I live without my darling Anne and my children?" My sister Anne lived. She had two more children, Joanne and Marie-Louise. Sadly, however, she never fully recovered from unremitting physical and mental suffering. In January 1980, she took her own life.

Oh, let us not be ashamed to weep at the "pitiableness of it all." But tears and weeping are mere self-indulgence if they don't move us to act for peace and justice.

Responding to this tragedy, and the previous death of sixteen hundred people over the first seven years of the Troubles, the Peace People movement was started. Fourteen years later, we are a small organization, doing what we can, as best we can. We feel privileged to be part of an ever-growing overall movement for nonviolence, justice, and reconciliation in Northern Ireland.

We know, too, the need to work in solidarity with the growing number of people around the world who are committing their lives to building a peaceful, healthy planet.

In the last decade, there has been a tremendous increase in the number of groups working nonviolently for social, political, and environmental changes. We rejoice and celebrate to be living in an age when miracles and wonders are unfolding before our very eyes. Indeed, there are so many groups and organizations that peacemakers often find it difficult to choose how and where best to use their talents and energy in order to create a peaceful planet. Here it may be helpful to remember the prayer of Catherine de Vinck: "Help me to forge ahead and to be true to my own nature without being hindered by false assumptions of the past or by passing fads of the present."

It would be a tragedy if peacemakers chose to work solely on the symptoms of violence or fads of the present day, instead of tackling the root cause of violence. What then is the root cause of violence? Thomas Merton wrote "that the root of humanity's problem is that its conscience is all fouled up and it does not appreciate reality as it fully and really is: in ways that are prejudiced and predetermined to fit a certain wrong picture of the world, in which humanity exists as an individual ego at the center of things." Merton goes on to say that "this experience of ourselves, as absolutely autonomous individual egos, is the source of all our problems."

Surely, then, if the root of the problem is a "dulled" or

"dead" conscience, the peacemaker must begin the hard work of peace in her or his conscience. Here we allow God to strip away all illusions and prejudices, so we can begin to know ourselves as we truly are. We begin to know it is an illusion to think that we are a separate existence. We realize that we are one with other people and with our universe.

We must not make the mistake of thinking that it is far more important to work on urgent political issues rather than make the time to pray that the greed, selfishness, hate, fear, and murderous anger that lie hidden in all our hearts are replaced with love, peace, joy, wisdom, perseverance, and kindness.

As Christian peacemakers, we can fast and pray to God to restore us to wholeness. God's desire with our consent is to uproot the violence within us and root us in Christ's nonviolence.

How do we define this nonviolence? Fr. Charlie McCarthy defines it as "giving up the protection of violence; stopping our use of violence; and stopping the hurting of other people." Fr. Dominique Barbé says, "It's a form of combativeness that's very original and powerful. Nonviolence is not just individual. It has a social and political character. It has a revolutionary aspect in that its end is to transform society."

To find out what nonviolence means, we Christians turn to the Scriptures and the life of Christ, who says, "I am the way." In the Scriptures we find nonviolent love in action. In the Eucharist, too, we find Jesus, the God who is love, giving love totally and unconditionally to each one of us. Nothing any one of us does can make God love us more or less. No matter how much wrong we do, God goes on loving and leaving the way open for us to repent. God's divine plan is to impregnate us with love, to make us God-like, so that we too can love humanity and creation with perfect divine love.

The Eucharistic sacrifice is completed at the crucifixion, when Jesus dies a victim of the sin of violence. Right to the end, Jesus rejects violence. His message is clear: love your enemies, forgive one another.

The gospels tell us that beside the cross stood Mary, the mother of Jesus. Could we women in the Christian peace movement have a more inspiring, courageous, role model than Mary, the Mother of Nonviolence? Mary, standing silently, prayerfully, in the shadow of the cross, is a powerful symbol of nonviolent love. She was not complaining about the injustice of it all, and what could be more unjust than the death of her own innocent son? No, she was praying with Jesus for repentance and forgiveness for us all. That was her role at the foot of the cross.

At another time, she spoke bravely for justice. In the Magnificat, she proclaimed justice for the poor and the oppressed. "God has shown the power of God's arm. God has routed the proud-hearted. God has pulled down princes from their thrones and exalted the poor and lowly. The hungry God has filled with good things and the rich God has sent empty away" (Luke 1:51–53).

Scripture tells us that John the beloved disciple stood by the cross of Jesus. John gives us a beautiful example of nonviolent action. He refused to give in to fear, to allow evil to go unchallenged and do nothing. Instead he stood and challenged this evil with his quiet, prayerful presence. This is the most powerful testimony to truth we can make, to put our lives on the line and to be prepared to die rather than to kill, like Jesus, Mary, and John on the hill of Calvary, two thousand years ago.

Choosing Jesus' way of nonviolence is for us Christians not simply a matter of being faithful to the gospel. It also meets humanity's need for an alternative to violence. Nonviolence needs to be taught at every level in every society.

In Northern Ireland, we know the need for learning an alternative to violence both at personal and structural levels. Our society is a victim of violence, the violence that comes from fear, hatred, and domination. There are two communities, and they fear domination by one section of the community over the other. This fear leads to anger and violence. The denial of equal rights for the minority community is another major factor.

In Northern Ireland there is a great deal of state-sanctioned injustice. The British government has removed many basic human rights. The restoration of these human rights is a priority if the people are to move forward to dialogue, reconciliation, and nonviolence. If the government upholds human rights and participates in dialogue with all parties involved, then we will start down the path to peace.

The church's and the Christian peacemaker's best contribution to a peaceful world is to be faithful to their own mission to teach and live as clearly as possible Jesus' message of nonviolent love for enemies.

In a world of believers and seekers, we are challenged to seek out new institutions and structures of society, built not on violence, but on respect for life and creation. This will enable humanity to move forward creatively together. Then we will fulfill our social and political responsibilities by playing our part in the development of a better world for all.

In their working document on nonviolence, Pax Christi International writes: "The fact that nonviolent defense as a socially organized way of resolving conflict is still in its infancy should not deter us from striving to understand it and promote it as an alternative to the generally accepted methods of conflict resolution, particularly as an alternative to defense by contemporary methods of warfare and deterrence. Organized civilian-based defense consisting of planned nonviolent strategies and tactics by citizens trained in nonviolent struggle deserves more study and consideration than has hitherto been given to it. The ways of war rely on the willingness and ability to dominate one's opponent by inflicting unacceptable levels of damage to life and property. Nonviolent approaches to security, on the other hand, can best be understood as a new and radical stage in human maturity, a step toward methods of conflict resolution in keeping with our vocation as children of God, made in God's image.

"Clearly the translation of nonviolence as a vision to nonviolence as a way of life and political strategy is neither automatic nor easy," Pax Christi continues. "A major task facing the human race today is the professionalization of humane ways of settling political conflicts, both within and between states."

We peacemakers are on a long pilgrimage. Where will we get the strength to persevere in our work?

I once asked Mother Teresa for her advice to me about being a peacemaker. She said simply, "Pray. Pray all the time. Never cease to pray." That was the best piece of advice I ever received. The rosary, the Eucharist, and our times of meditation are our great strength. There we receive peace and joy and the knowledge that success is not our business, that we are called only to do our best and to persevere. God will, in God's good time, do the rest.

We can be encouraged by the example of Cardinal Newman. When speaking about the role of the laity in the church, Cardinal Newman said, "What I aim at may be real and good, but it may be God's will that it should be done a hundred years later." Almost exactly one hundred years later, Newman's ideas on the role of the laity in the church found expression in the decrees of the Second Vatican Council.

Newman had a dream. Your own great prophet, Martin Luther King, Jr., had a dream. I too have a dream of a time when human life is held as so sacred that no one can kill, when justice will reign in every heart and in every land. Wars will cease and no one will have too much while others have nothing.

Our God has a dream. "God calls humanity to be like God, all love," Jean Goss writes. "God is love. God has dreamed an incredible dream, to make men and women like God's own self, free, beautiful, good, pure, filled with strength and love. Yes, God wants to make himself one with them! To give himself completely."

We are all God's children. Our God asks us to become as little children. As peace-seekers, as little children, let us allow God to fulfill this great dream in us. We only have to consent, like our Blessed Lady did. Then the Holy Spirit will fill us with God's love for humanity and creation. This is God's way to create a peaceful planet. So with the confidence, joy, and trust of little children, let us say, "Yes, Yes, Yes," to God's beautiful dream for you, for me, and for all humanity.

Let us recommit ourselves to the power of nonviolence and "join with the earth and each other, to bring new life to the land, to restore the world, to refresh the air, to renew the forests, to care for the plants, to protect the creatures, to celebrate the seas, to rejoice in the sunlight, to sing the song of the stars, to recall our destiny, to renew our spirits, to reinvigorate our bodies, to recreate the human community, to promote justice and peace, to love our children and one another, to join together as many diverse expressions of one loving mystery, for the healing of the earth and the renewal of all life."*

---

*Quote from Fr. Ted Hesburgh, speech at Stamford, Connecticut, October 9, 1991.

22

The Peacemaking Church

Many people around the world claim that religion is the problem in Northern Ireland. For those of us who live here, however, we know that the Troubles have deep social, economic, cultural, historical, and political roots. But we admit that religion plays an important role in our society and is, therefore, also part of the problem.

How can our church become part of the solution in Northern Ireland? I would like to consider the three different forms of church and how it can be part of the solution.

First, the parish. As there is a great deal of violence and suffering in Northern Ireland and it has lasted for such a long time, people need hope. The church can offer spiritual, prophetic leadership to the people of God. It can be a sign of hope. Because we are Christians living in dark days, the spirit of Christ and the vision he laid out for the people of God, a life of peace, love, and reconciliation, the beloved kingdom of God on earth, have never been more urgent than for the people of Northern Ireland. The church can help develop its people spiritually, to become loving and compassionate so they can build a compassionate society.

The church is well placed to build such communities through its parishes by challenging the people of God to be true to the message of Jesus. I believe the Sermon on the Mount is a call for Christians to live nonviolence in their daily lives and to change unjust structures and institutions through the power of truth and love according to the example given by the nonviolent Jesus. I believe the most powerful contribution toward solving individual, community, and world problems that the church can make is to teach nonviolence to Christians. We have the greatest model for challenging evil in the life of Jesus, especially in his death on the cross and his refusal to take human life.

Perhaps some of the following steps may be of help:

1. Schools and communities can study early Christian history, especially the first three centuries, when Christians re-

Previously unpublished.

fused to kill for any military institution and emphasized the commands to love our enemies and be reconciled.

2. Clergy can begin to share power and decision-making with the laity and thereby encourage partnerships in parish councils.

3. We can create new structures which will empower and encourage the laity to participate more fully in the church, to cooperate and take new responsibilities. The sharing of power will develop greater respect for the individual and allow for the growth of creativity and new energy.

4. We can encourage equality of the sexes, the service of altar girls, sermons by lay men and women, and equal participation in all parish roles. Ageism and racism can be discouraged by the active involvement of older parishioners and people from different races in all activities.

5. We can encourage accountability on all levels, including full financial reports to parishioners.

6. The practice of sending retired priests to country parishes should be reassessed. Also, younger lay men and women could be trained to work alongside older priests to help share the workload, especially home visitations in rural areas.

7. Clergy can encourage an inclusive attitude toward all people, especially those from different religious denominations, and more inclusive language so that we no longer speak of "us vs. them," but we-we.

8. The clergy can help by emphasizing that the human person is the most sacred value in society and that we should not put the false gods of money, job, or country, before God and human life.

9. We should acknowledge the right of parents to choose whichever type of education they want for their children, including integrated education (Catholic and Protestant schools). Integrated education offers a practical way for our children to learn about each other, and those who choose to send their children to such schools should be supported.

10. Clergy can encourage ecumenism, explaining the importance of respect for other faiths and denominations. We need to challenge the destructive idea that Catholics are "disloyal" if they question their church or participate in worship services in other denominations. Clergy could be proactive in encouraging parishioners to participate in services of other reli-

gious denominations. Ecumenical days or shared church events
help to build trust and respect for diversity.

11. Eucharistic sharing is one important way for Christian
people to grow together and should not be refused to those
who wish to share at the Eucharistic table of Christ.

12. Where there is rivalry, enmity, and animosity between
local churches, and even parishes, interparish and interchurch
links become urgent. We need to create more opportunities for
sharing and common worship so that people can get to know
each other in an enjoyable and relaxing atmosphere. Then our
church will reflect the peace we seek.

cᐧ∞ᐧ

Second, the institutional church. The deeper problem of classism, the great divide between the working class and the middle
class in Northern Ireland, is just as much a challenge to the
churches as the Catholic/Protestant division. The anger, fear,
and hatred between classes can be changed only through compassion and a recognition that each person has a right to life and
the pursuit of happiness. As Christians we have a responsibility to work for the happiness of others. We are challenged to
seek the Kingdom of God here on earth by working for social,
economic, and political justice.

Hatred and violence grow out of injustice, alienation, depri-
vation, and oppression. To remove violence, we must remove
injustice. The church can do much to educate people about the
connection between peace and justice.

Although the Catholic Church is a teaching church, we still
do not have a theology of peace and justice. Some people in
Northern Ireland today who believe they are fighting a just war
believe that the Catholic Church blesses "just wars." I believe
the Catholic Church could make an enormous contribution
to peace in Ireland by publicly renouncing the just war theory
and developing a theology of nonviolence in keeping with the
teaching and life of Jesus.

We are often told that as individual Catholics we are the
church. Jesus came to liberate individuals, but in order to liberate individuals, there must be a real change in the institutional
church. Until the church hierarchy recognizes that through
baptism men and women are equal before God and recognizes
this equality in their institutional framework, men will con-

tinue to control all church ministries. The movements in the last centuries — the women's, human rights, nonviolence, and democracy movements — challenge old attitudes and institutions around the world. People are becoming more confident and empowered. When they find institutions or organizations that do not uphold the individual and encourage empowerment, they become disillusioned and move away. I believe we are witnessing such a movement, especially in the younger generation, who are finding fulfillment in alternative movements. Young people are refusing to be dominated. They will not accept authoritarian, bureaucratic, indoctrinating systems. Today as never before, people realize that classism, racism, sexism, exploitation, violence, and war are demonic. Systems which dominate and destroy human growth are in need of change.

The institutional church needs to change. The Spirit of Jesus, the light of hope and nonviolence, must be allowed to shine. This spirit of respect for each person, this spirit of inclusiveness, equality, harmony, solidarity, partnership, responsibility, and flexibility must be practiced within our church if we will draw people together in love. The institutional church must practice peace at all levels as it grows to become a peacemaking church.

ᕁ

Third, on the personal level, it is important to look at the roots of our own intolerance and try to change ourselves. We need to be aware of our negative words and actions, as well as learn to listen to others and be open to dialogue based on respect. We need to speak our love and respect to one another, to speak honestly about how we feel about important matters and to listen carefully to how others perceive these matters. No one has a monopoly on truth. We need each other for a fuller and deeper perspective on reality in our common pursuit of truth.

In the final analysis, each one of us is the church. Each one of us can try to live according to our own informed conscience and through our prayer, strive to have a mind of love and compassion. When we recognize that our real enemies are hatred and anger, that they block compassion, we will work to remove these obstacles from our minds and allow God to make us, the whole church, into a part of the solution. In that spirit of nonviolence, we will become a peacemaking church.

23

All Life Is Sacred

The First Declaration of Human Rights was written in August 1789. Since that time two hundred years ago, humankind has made giant steps forward in many sciences, and particularly in technology. However, we have only taken small steps in the development and respect of human rights, on the individual and social levels.

Throughout the world, millions of people live without basic human rights. Young children die of starvation and disease, even while our acquired knowledge has made it possible for us to grant them the basic human right of food. One big difference between 1789 and 1989 is that we now have the knowledge to fulfill many basic human rights, but we lack the political will necessary to implement them.

For millions of our sisters and brothers, particularly in the Third World, life is unbearably painful. For those of us who live in Western countries, we can never begin to imagine the horror of waiting helplessly while one's little child slowly dies of hunger. In a world filled with suffering, we all need to have faith and hope that such injustice in our world will be changed. Faith and hope are as important to our spirit as food is to our body. But to the human eye, such change looks impossible. From where shall our hope come?

Hope springs alive and grows as we become increasingly conscious of the gift of God's presence and love, and conscious too of the astonishing reality that we are both the "receivers and givers" of this miraculous power of life-giving, healing love. Hope springs alive when we know we are loved and when we begin to love others. This love leads us to see God, not in the heavens, but in every human being, especially in the poor and suffering. It enables us to respect every person. Unconditional love has the power to change everything. We are called to that love.

This reflection was offered as a contribution to the 1989 French Association "Artists '89" exhibition entitled "International Images for the Rights of Humanity and Citizens," which was distributed throughout the world in celebration of the bicentenary of the French Revolution.

So too we are called to be seekers and speakers of truth. Let us seek and speak of a Great Truth. One Great Truth is that "all life is sacred and no one has the right to take life." All men and women know instinctively that their own life is sacred and would never allow anyone the right to take away their life. It follows then that this right belongs to all, and the "Right to Life" is the first and most important of all human rights.

The most serious threat to this first of all human rights, the right to life, is the lie that there are circumstances when violence, torture, homicide, wars, and even nuclear weapons are necessary and even moral. This lie is helped by the misguided arguments of some who claim that humankind is by nature violent and things can never be changed. Not so. Yes, every human being has two options — acting violently or acting nonviolently. But our societies do not encourage but rather hinder people from overcoming the drive for violence by seeking truth through loving means instead. A great effort must be made to help diminish and overcome violence in each individual, in society, and in the world.

Killing is against our nature. War is a "taught" evil. We can change all this. Individuals can refuse to kill their fellow human beings. We can say No to any and every form of violence, individually and socially.

We are challenged to replace the law of violence with the law of love. We can say No when our countries spend our money on death machines to "protect" us from "threats" which often do not exist. We can say No to the culture of death and its militarism which saps the creative energy of our youth. Instead of providing real security, such militarism actually creates a climate of fear.

Security is never found in the possession of guns and stockpiles of weapons. In reality, we can never have total security. We are vulnerable. By accepting our vulnerability and trusting in our God, we can be released from the terrible fear which drives us to build and maintain more and more weapons and to maintain "an armed security." There are many ways we can diminish this false security and develop the real security of peace. We can build trusting relationships which lead to genuine reconciliation among all peoples. When we acknowledge that we have hurt one another and ask for each other's forgiveness, reconciliation occurs, and we can dismantle our weapons and live

in peace. As we recognize and accept the uniqueness and origi-
nality of each culture, agree not to kill one another, try to share
our resources equally, and deepen our ongoing dialogue, we
can make the world a truly secure place.

Real security develops as we identify and pick up the common threads between cultures and countries and knit them
together for the welfare of humanity. The commitment to the
poor may be the most important thread that draws all the diverse cultures and countries together. Our concern for the poor
and our efforts to meet all their needs will lead us on the way
to a more peaceful, just world. I think of Mohammed's prayer.
"Allah, let me pass my life as poor among the poor. Let me die
among the poor and on the day of resurrection raise me from
among the poor." If we all adopt this attitude, we will find
ourselves united.

The world's governments need to divert the money they
pour into militarism into development projects for the hungry
and the poor at home and around the world and systematically
work to abolish hunger, disease, homelessness, poverty, pollu-
tion, and all the other evils which are the real enemies of the
human family.

In order to bring about the necessary changes in our societies
and in our world, superficial structural and economic changes,
though critically essential, are still not enough. What is needed
is a complete change of consciousness. As we recognize that
we are connected with all people, with the whole world and
indeed the universe, we realize that the ultimate challenge is
to live together in a new way where we respect all life and all
creation. We will have to undergo a "Damascus conversion"
like Saul who becomes Paul, a conversion from killing to love,
from militarism to nonviolence. Some people work for the
abolition of war and nuclear weapons out of fear. But it will
not be the fear of nuclear weapons or our economic necessity
that finally brings about disarmament and justice. Our common conscience and our faith in a loving God will lead us to
realize that it is wrong to kill another human being. Then we
will all rededicate ourselves to the service of suffering humanity
and peace.

If we choose to live nonviolently, we will have to do more
than pledge never to kill another. Our nonviolence must push
us to reject every weapon of mass destruction, every war,

and every gun right down to the refusal even to slight another person. This way of active nonviolence will enable us to change our unjust political structures and redistribute the world's goods equally. From now on, we will uphold the sanctity of life and treat everyone with the deepest respect.

Even when we deal with those who do wrong, we will show respect and win them over. It is only through respect that it is possible to release the inherent goodness and greatness within every human being.

24

The Meaning of Life

I have life. With little effort on my behalf, apart from feeding my body, life pulsates through me. I have a body and a soul. I know that at some point, physical life will be taken from me and my body will die. However, my soul, which has been created by God, can never die. By the power and mystery of God's grace, God's spirit of love lives in every human soul. We are loved by God, and we are created to love God, to see the Spirit of God in every person and to love and serve others.

There are many gifts that are given along with life, but the jewels among them are free will and love. With free will come choice and responsibility. We must daily make very important choices. We can choose between life or death, good or evil, love or hate. We can choose to be creators or destroyers of life.

Personally, I choose to live. I know that my life and all human life is sacred and precious. This means that I must never kill another person and must reject personal and social violence.

But it is not enough to refuse to kill. God's gift of love opens our hearts to see that the real enemies of humankind are disease, hunger, homelessness, poverty, greed, torture, and war. We must work to change these injustices.

Through active nonviolence, we can work for justice, especially for the suffering and the poor. Through truth and love, we can change ourselves and our world, and come to know more deeply that we are born to love and to be loved.

Published by *Life* magazine in the book *The Meaning of Life*, 1991.

25

Merton's Advice

Recently, Peace People friends and members came together to celebrate our anniversary and to rededicate ourselves to the work for peace. On that occasion, a journalist asked me, "What results or successes have the Peace People had?"

This question reminded me of Thomas Merton's advice to peacemakers, when he cautioned them not to make the mistake of becoming "success oriented" and fail to recognize that the diseases we struggle against might be too complex and too far advanced for us. He felt that insisting on evidence of success might quickly lead us to despair and paralysis.

"Do not depend on the hope of results," Merton wrote. "When you are doing the sort of work you have taken on, essentially an apostolic work, you have to face the fact that the work will be apparently worthless and achieve no result at all, if not perhaps results opposite to what you expect.

"As you get used to this idea, you start more and more to concentrate not on the results but on the value, the rightness, the truth of the work itself. And there too a great deal has to be gone through, as gradually you struggle less and less for an idea and more and more for specific people. The range tends to narrow down, but it gets much more real. In the end, it is the reality of personal relationships that saves everything. The big results are not in your hands or mine, but they suddenly happen, and we can share in them; but there is no point in building our lives on this personal satisfaction, which may be denied to us and which after all is not that important."*

At the beginning of the Peace People movement, some of us started out to change Northern Ireland and the world. In the years since, I have come to believe that the real struggle starts in my own heart and in all our own hearts and that "inner change" should be the first priority in life. Learning "to be still" and peaceful is our daily work, a lifetime's work, but it must be done. Otherwise, do we have anything to offer? If we our-

Published in *Peace by Peace,* Belfast, October 1986.

*From *The Hidden Ground of Love: The Letters of Thomas Merton,* vol. 1 (New York: Farrar, Straus, & Giroux, 1985), 294.

selves are full of tension, anger, and confusion, are we not only adding to the hurt and division around us?

Looking back now to the hectic, early months of the Peace People movement, I realize we were working all the time, day and night, under tremendous pressure. We were tired and irritable and often completely drained by committee meetings. I am sure that sometimes I said and did things that were not very peaceful for which I am sorry and hope I am forgiven. However, thank God, now we are not under those enormous pressures and we have more time, time which I believe we should use to pray and meditate that the spirit of peace and joy may permeate our whole being so that we may be "peace-creators" and not "peace-blockers."

I take real inspiration from Merton's insight that "in the end, it is the reality of personal relationships that saves everything." Merton put his finger on what is for me one of the "fruits" of the peace movement. My own life has been greatly enriched by the people whom I have had the privilege to know and work with and call "friends," both in the early years of the Peace People and today.

I know I am not the only one who feels deeply about these friendships. At the recent Peace People rededication ceremony, there were tears and moments of joy. We have come to treasure the personal relationships forged over the years working together for peace and justice. For some of us, our joy was a bit clouded by the absence of friends who we would have loved to be present with us and who were very much in our thoughts and prayers that day.

Our friend Alan Senior, for example, could not be with us that day because of his illness, and sadly he has since died and gone home to God. I know he will pray for us as I believe that friendships do not end with death but are connected by the spirit of love "till we all merrily meet in heaven." Alan was to me and to many other people a good friend, and perhaps the best tribute we can pay to his memory is to continue with the peace work where he left off, in a spirit of real friendship, "where we are prepared to give more of ourselves to listen to each other and above all, to learn to accept and be accepted by one another as we walk joyously along the road of peace together."

"In the end, it is the reality of personal relationships that saves everything."

26

A New Millennium of Nonviolence

I am happy to join the campaign of Nobel laureates on behalf of the children of the world. This campaign is an important step toward the building of a new culture of nonviolence for the human family.

To help build this culture of nonviolence, we appeal to all heads of state, all member countries of the United Nations, and the UN General Assembly:

- that the first decade of the new millennium, the years 2000–2010, be declared the "Decade for a Culture of Nonviolence";

- that at the start of the decade, the year 2000 be declared the "Year of Education for Nonviolence";

- and that nonviolence be taught at every level of our societies during this decade, to make the children of the world aware of the real, practical meaning and benefits of nonviolence in their daily lives, in order to reduce the violence and consequent suffering perpetrated against them and humanity in general.

We live in a wonderful world. There is much to celebrate and give thanks for. But we also live in an increasingly violent world. Tragically, violence in its many forms is still acceptable as a way of dealing with each other. The culture of violence is taking hold in more and more of our societies, and it is all too often seen as inevitable. It is important that we do all in our power to reverse this thinking and begin to think in a whole new way.

Comments at a press conference in Paris, France, July 1, 1997, at the release of a statement calling for a new millennium of nonviolence signed by twenty Nobel Peace Prize winners, including Mother Teresa, Desmond Tutu, Nelson Mandela, Aung San Suu Kyi, the Dalai Lama, Elie Wiesel, Mikhail Gorbachev, Shimon Peres, Adolfo Pérez Esquivel, Yasir Arafat, Bishop Belo, José Ramos Horta, Oscar Arias, Willem deKlerk, Betty Williams, Lech Walesa, and Joseph Rotblat. For further information on the UN "Decade of Nonviolence," contact the Fellowship of Reconciliation, Box 271, Nyack, NY 10960, (914) 358-4601.

Violence is not inevitable. Nonviolence, the spirit of love and compassion, lives in the hearts of all men and women. It is this spirit we must evoke and awaken. We need to empower one another to work together to change from a culture of violence to a culture of nonviolence.

All the children of the world have a right to a better future. But this can be assured only through the self-sacrifice, dedication, hard work, and courage of us all.

All the children of the world have a right to peace and happiness, but this can be assured only through the rejection of the bomb, the bullet, and all the techniques of violence, accepted by so many today.

To enable peace to flourish in the hearts of our young people, it is urgent that we begin to teach nonviolence everywhere, including in our homes and in our schools. These techniques will provide young people with the tools to begin to solve their problems through dialogue and negotiation. They will create an ethos whereby the use of violence becomes unnecessary, unacceptable, and unthinkable.

Nonviolence — the respect of all life and the environment — is both taught and caught. We teach English and math and expect our children to read and calculate. As we enter the third millennium, is it not time that we begin to teach nonviolence in our classrooms and our homes as well?

In creating a culture of nonviolence, the world's religions have an important role to play. Did not all the founders of the great religions by their lives and examples teach respect for life, compassion, and the basis for a nonviolent lifestyle?

Indeed, this great challenge cannot be left to only a few. Everyone has a role to play in the creation of a culture of nonviolence.

Therefore, we invite all men and women, all boys and girls, to join us in this great campaign to reject all forms of violence and to build a culture of peace, nonviolence, and justice throughout our world. Let us proclaim to all the world with all our hearts that peace is a right of all the world's children and that, if we work hard together in a spirit of love and compassion, it will be possible for them all to have peace and happiness.

Together we can build a new culture of nonviolence for humankind which will give hope to all humanity and, in particular, to the children of the world.

Epilogue

The agreement signed on Good Friday, April 10, 1998, was a welcome first step toward building real peace and democracy in Ireland, North and South.

The agreement set new institutional and constitutional arrangements comprising an Assembly in Northern Ireland, a North/South Ministerial Council, implementation bodies, a British/Irish Council and a British/Irish Inter-governmental Conference, together with amendments to British Acts of Parliament and the Constitution of Ireland. It also includes a Justice and Human Rights program.

I believe this agreement was fair and balanced, and while not everyone can agree with everything, there was something for everyone in it.

No one should underestimate the real achievements this agreement means, and tribute must rightly be paid to all those who helped bring it about. The courage, determination, and commitment of President Clinton, his envoy and chairman of the talks, Senator Mitchell, Secretary of State Dr. Mo Mowlam, the British and Irish prime ministers, and the politicians must be acknowledged.

It took enormous courage for many of these politicians (traditional opponents) to sit down together, agree to discard some long-held dogmatic principles, and accept compromise and change.

It took enormous courage for them to recognize each other's "identity" and agree to each person's right to different political aspirations.

It took enormous courage to agree to be inclusive rather than exclusive.

It took enormous courage to admit that violence is not the way forward and to pledge themselves to nonviolence and democracy.

When this agreement was reached by the politicians, it was a real sea-change in our politics. It was a consensus agreement — the first ever to be reached by age-old protagonists. It was above all an agreement to accept change.

All those involved, particularly the two prime ministers together with Northern Ireland's politicians, have given real

121

leadership. When it was put to the people of Ireland, North and South, for a referendum on May 22, 1998, it won over-whelming approval, with 72 percent of the people of Northern Ireland voting Yes.

We congratulate John Hume and David Trimble for win-ning the 1998 Nobel Peace Prize for their work for peace. And though we mourn the deaths of the three Quinn children and all those killed in the horrific Omagh bombing in the summer of 1998, we are still hopeful that a new era of peace is coming.

Here in Northern Ireland, we are being called upon to change. We are being challenged to change both ourselves and our society by the proposals in the Good Friday agreement. Most of us are afraid to change. We like the safety and security of "the way things are." Yes, change is painful, but when accepted gra-ciously, it allows us to grow spiritually. Change is inevitable. It is part of being human. I keep thinking of John Henry Newman's insight: "In a higher world, it is otherwise, but here below, to live is to change and to be perfect is to have changed often."

A positive approach to change gives us the confidence in our-selves to let go of fear, to reach out to others, and to be open to the creative possibilities which change can bring in the future.

Some opposed the Good Friday agreement because hun-dreds of convicted prisoners will be released within a few years. It is understandable that some of the families who have lost or had injured loved ones are feeling unhappy and upset about this. I am glad that the agreement acknowledged their feelings and offered support to such families who have suffered so much over the last thirty years. However, I do not believe that the victims' families should dictate the future of the prisoners, nor would most of them want to do so. Furthermore, it is deeply offensive when some politicians presume to speak on behalf of the victims' families and use their sufferings as a way to score political points. I personally welcome the agreement's approach toward dealing with the prisoners. While some fear that the prisoners will be a threat to the community, it is a fact that only a few ex-prisoners have ever reoffended, and most do not re-join paramilitary groups after their release. Many organizations, including the Peace People, have been enriched by the con-tributions that ex-prisoners have made within the community, especially their strong commitment to peace and reconciliation within Northern Ireland.

It is important to acknowledge that we have all been hurt over the years, that we have hurt each other, and that prisoners and their families have also suffered. More than anything, we are in need of forgiveness. I believe this is a key to building a genuine reconciled and healed community. Forgiveness does not come easy. It is a long, hard process. People are not being asked to forget the past, but rather to make a choice to forgive and move forward into a new future.

Forgiveness is the only way to personal peace. Even after "justice" has been done, many families have felt they needed something "more." Then they themselves chose to forgive and let go of their resentment. They released themselves from the need for punishment and revenge. Without forgiveness, there can be no real healing of ourselves, each other, or our community. Revenge keeps the violence circulating. Together with pride, the desire for revenge hardens our hearts against forgiveness. Punishment does not bring the victim inner peace of mind. Only the victim choosing to forgive can do that. Even after an offender has served a lifetime in prison, the victims often do not feel inner peace until they themselves make the decision to forgive.

Together with forgiveness, we also need acceptance. The Good Friday agreement is very complex, and it will take much hard work, commitment, good will, and cooperation by everyone in the years ahead to make it work. The most important ingredient is the will to make it work.

As we face the future, the question is raised: "Do the people of Northern Ireland will to make the agreement work?" They themselves are key players in these historic days. The Good Friday agreement offers the possibility of political stability, but it is we the people, in partnership with our chosen politicians, who will build a new society.

As we here in Northern Ireland take up the challenge to build together a culture of nonviolence and real democracy, we hope we will give encouragement to others around the world working for peace in their own countries.

As we enter the new millennium, I believe we can all take hope and inspiration from the knowledge that many, many millions of our sisters and brothers around the world are united in a spirit of solidarity and nonviolence and that, over time, the vision of peace will dawn in Northern Ireland and the world.

Mairead Corrigan Maguire, winner of the 1976 Nobel Peace Prize, is co-founder of the Community of the Peace People. For further information, contact:

Peace People
224 Lisburn Road
Belfast, Northern Ireland BT9 6GE
Tel. (1232) 663-465.
Fax. (1232) 683-947.
WEBsite: www.peacepeople.com

John Dear, S.J. is Executive Director of the Fellowship for Reconciliation, the largest, oldest, interfaith peace organization in the United States. For further information about FOR or to subscribe to *Fellowship* magazine, contact:

The Fellowship of Reconciliation
P.O. Box 271
Nyack, NY 10960, USA
Tel. (914) 358-4601
Fax. (914) 358-4924
WEBsite: www.nonviolence.org
E-mail: Fornatl@igc.apc.org